# The Adventures of Strawberryhead & Gingerbread

## Cursive Writing Workbook ③ of "Wacky" Dogs!

# The
# Adventures of
# Strawberryhead
# & Gingerbread
## Cursive Writing Workbook ③
## of "Wacky" Dogs!

KF Wheatie & KM Wheatie

Strawberryhead &
Gingerbread Press

www.strawberryheadandgingerbread.com

The Adventures of Strawberryhead & Gingerbread,

Cursive Writing Workbook ③ of *"Wacky"* Dogs!


Published by Strawberryhead and Gingerbread Press
https://www.strawberryheadandgingerbread.com

Copyright © 2024 by KF Wheatie & KM Wheatie




ISBN: 979-8-9894956-8-9

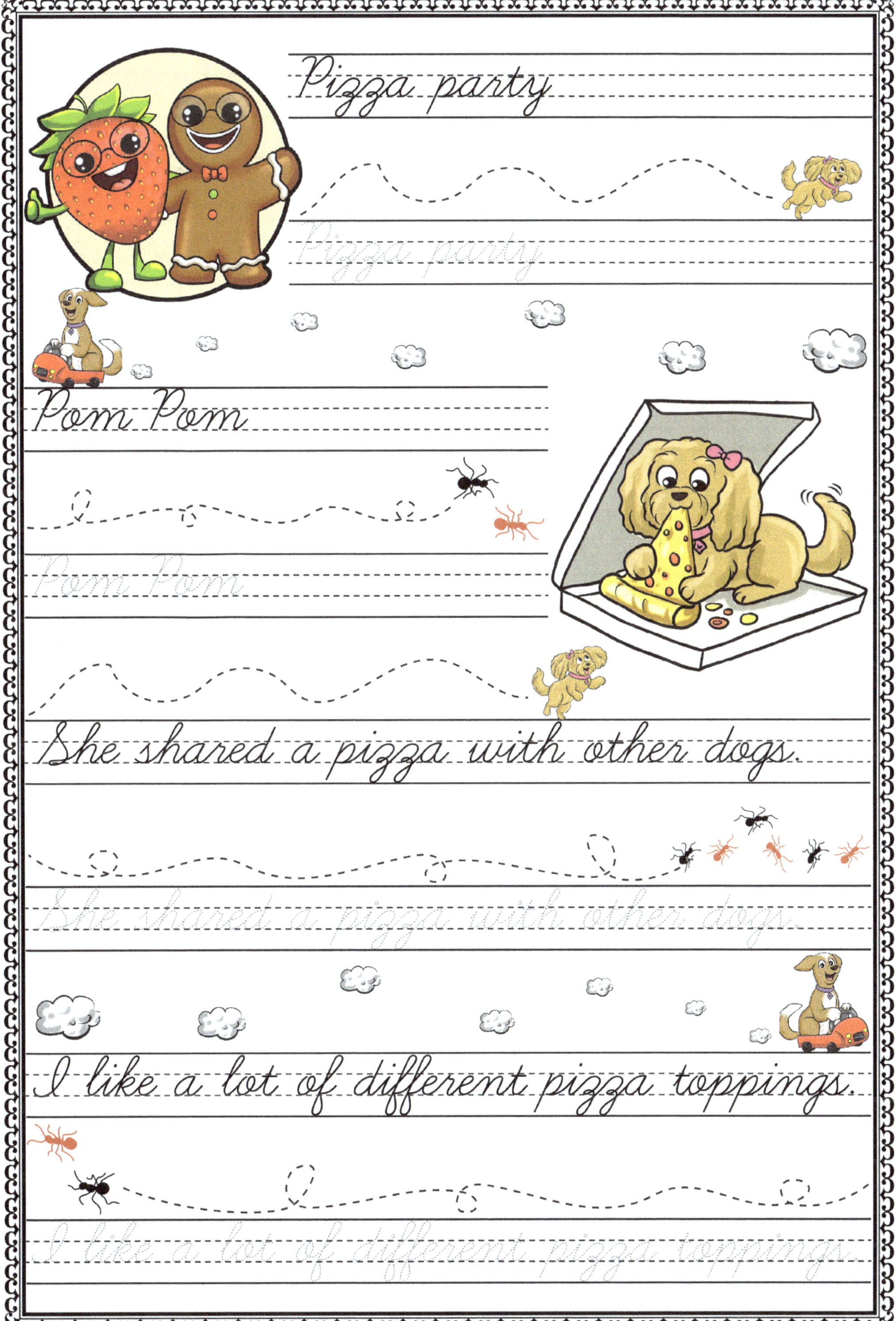

Pizza party

Pizza party

Pom Pom

Pom Pom

She shared a pizza with other dogs.

She shared a pizza with other dogs.

I like a lot of different pizza toppings.

I like a lot of different pizza toppings.

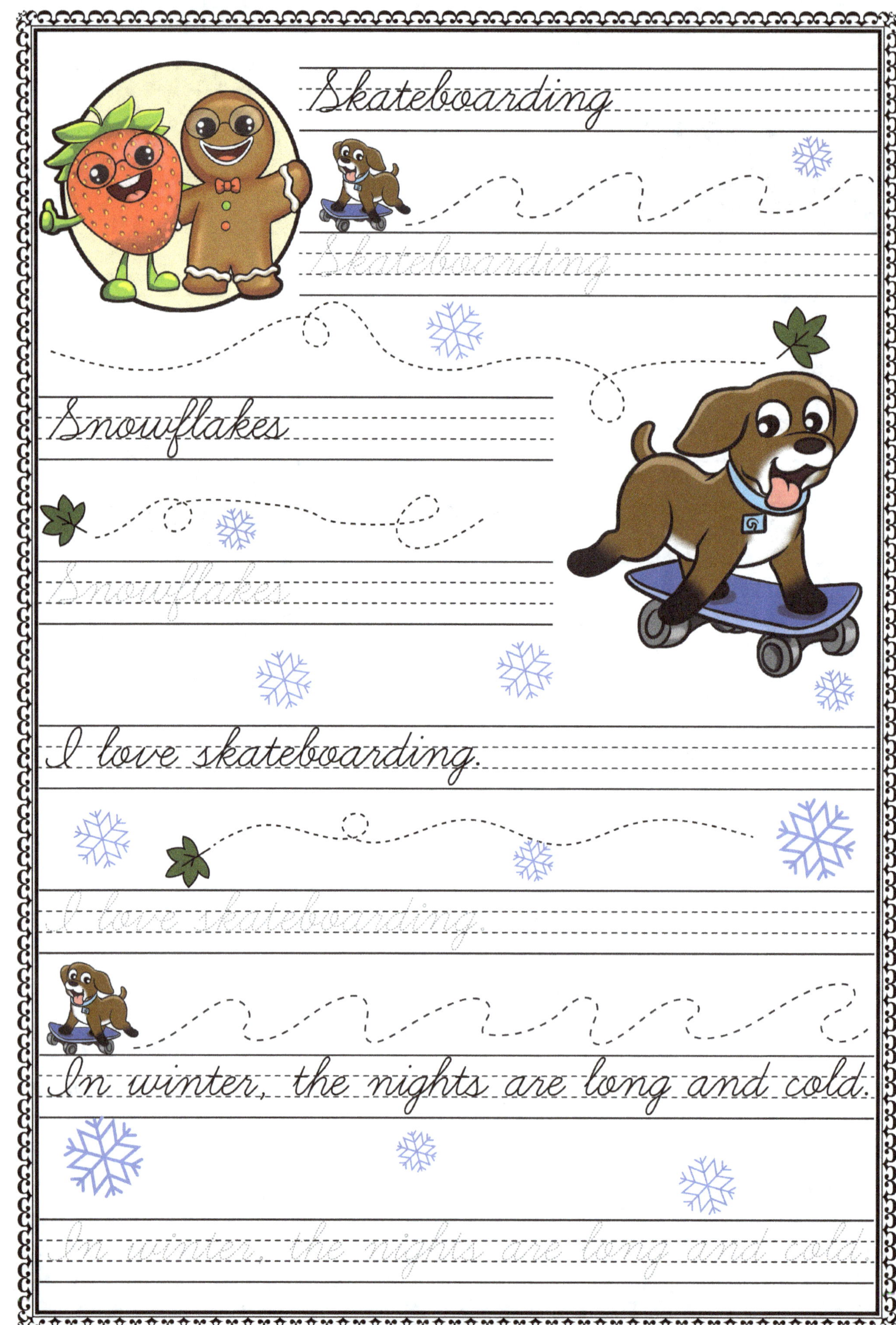

Skateboarding



Snowflakes



I love skateboarding.



In winter, the nights are long and cold.

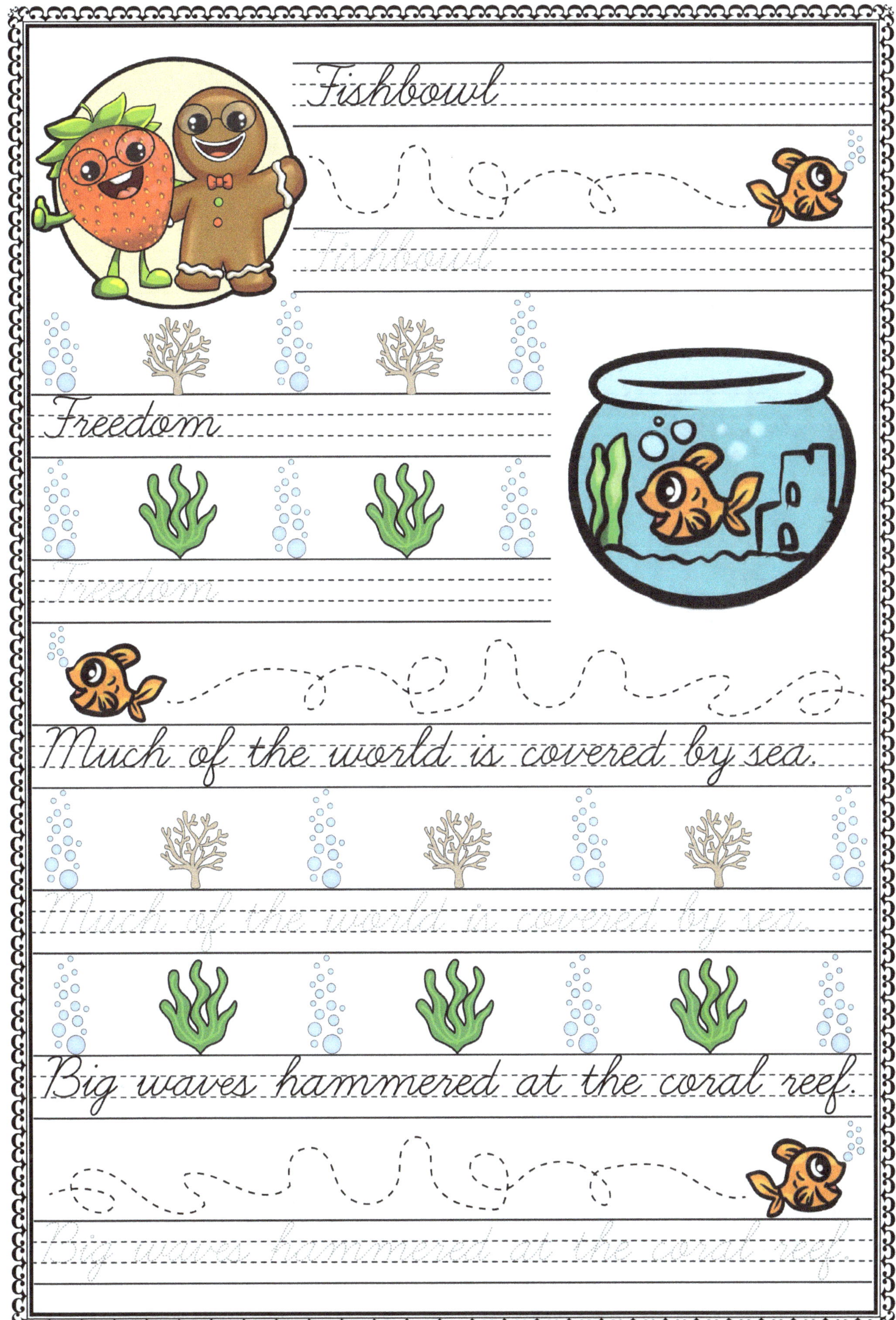

Fishbowl

Freedom

Much of the world is covered by sea.

Big waves hammered at the coral reef.

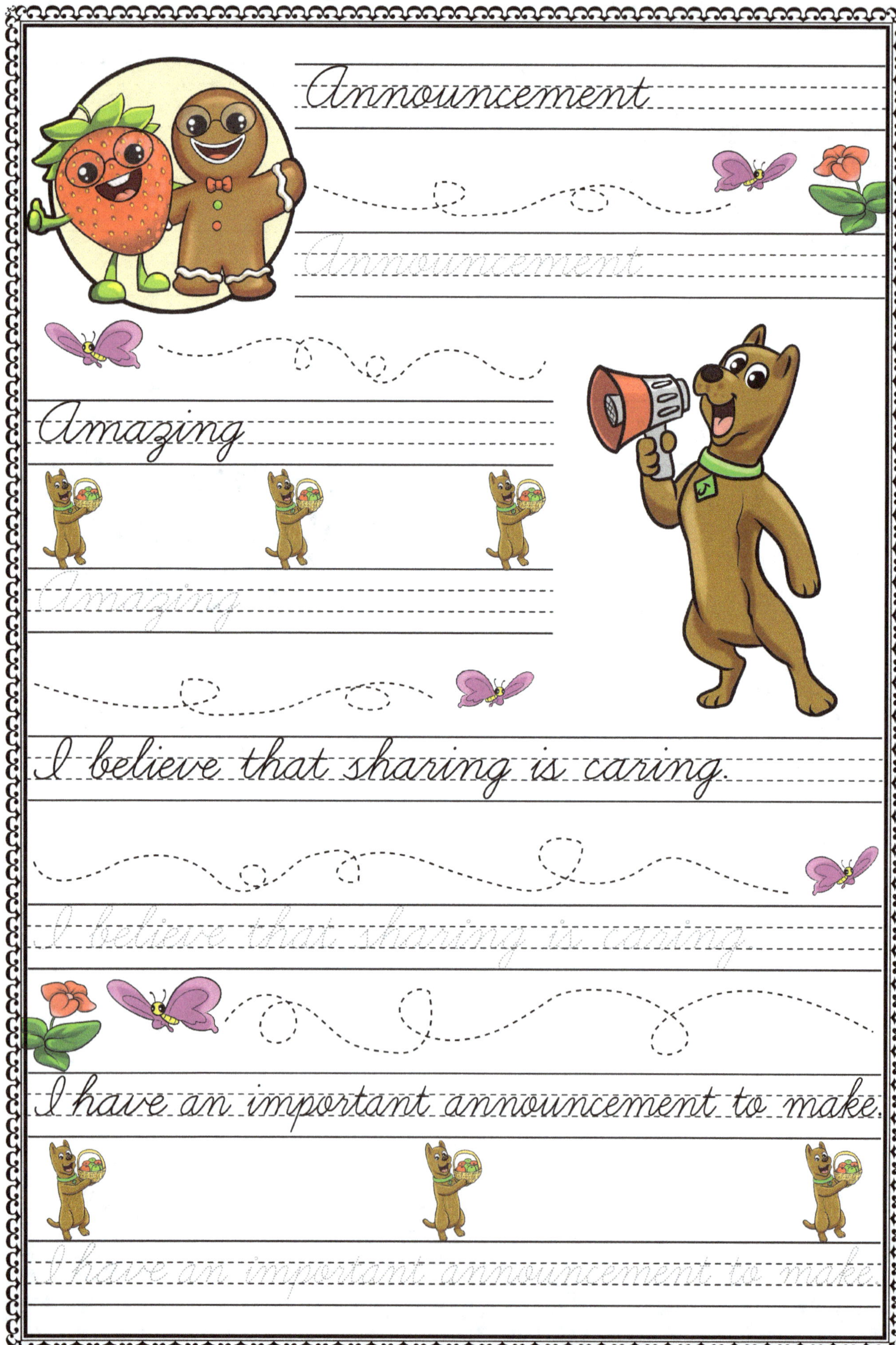

Announcement

Announcement

Amazing

Amazing

I believe that sharing is caring.

I believe that sharing is caring.

I have an important announcement to make.

I have an important announcement to make.

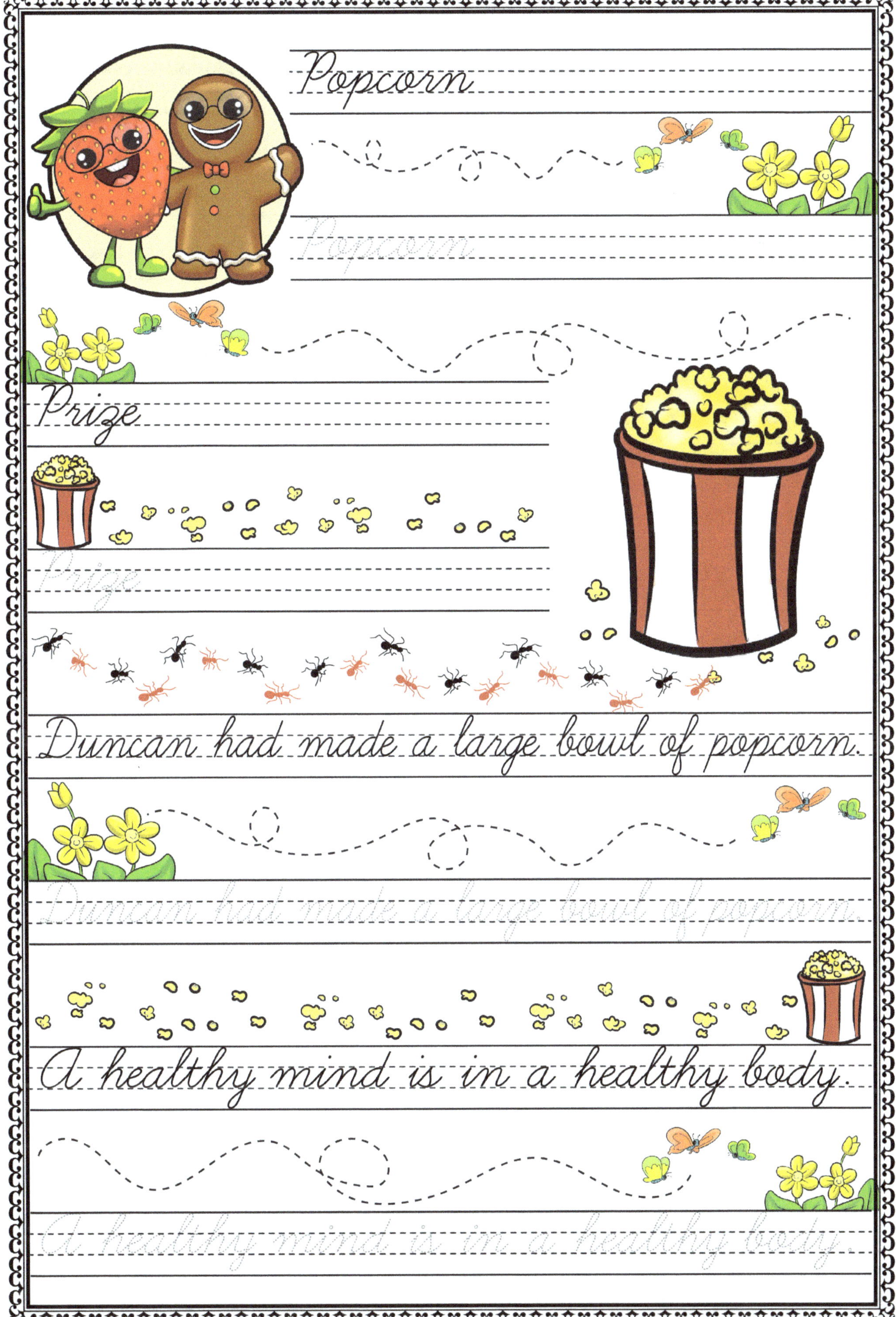

Popcorn

Prize

Duncan had made a large bowl of popcorn.

A healthy mind is in a healthy body.

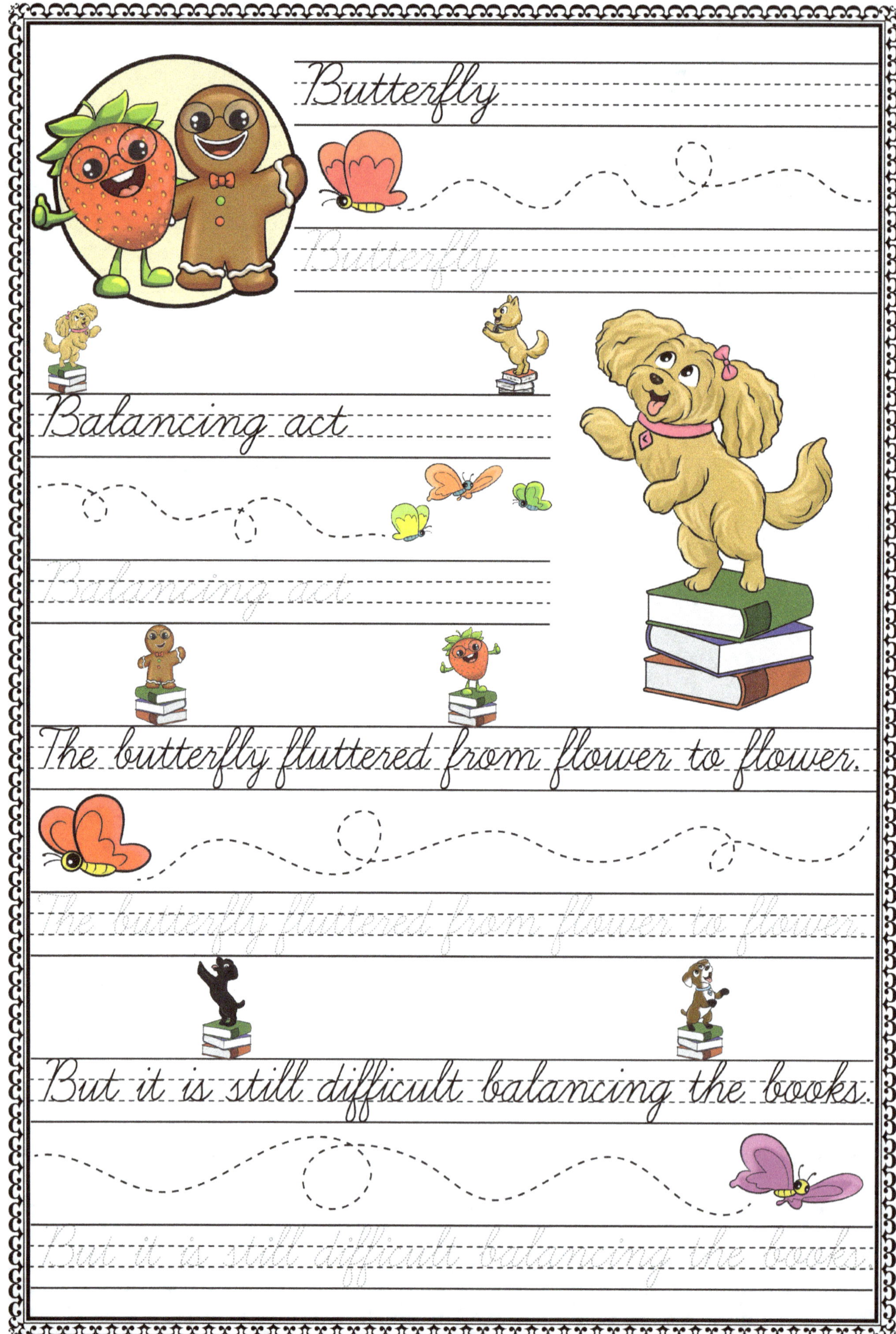


Butterfly
Butterfly
Balancing act
Balancing act
The butterfly fluttered from flower to flower.
The butterfly fluttered from flower to flower.
But it is still difficult balancing the books.
But it is still difficult balancing the books.

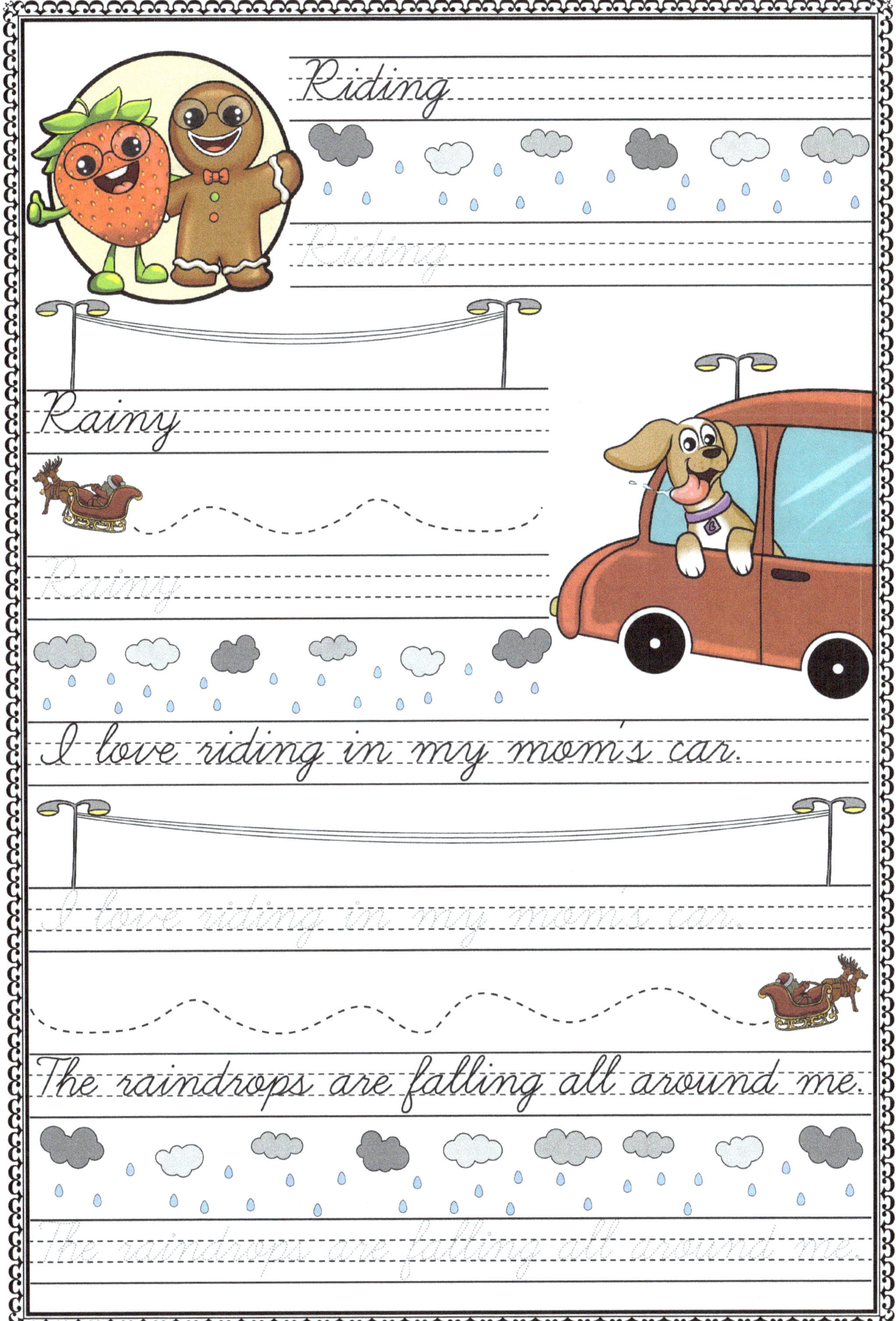

Riding

Riding

Rainy

Rainy

I love riding in my mom's car.

I love riding in my mom's car.

The raindrops are falling all around me.

The raindrops are falling all around me.

# Help Gingerbread reach Strawberryhead

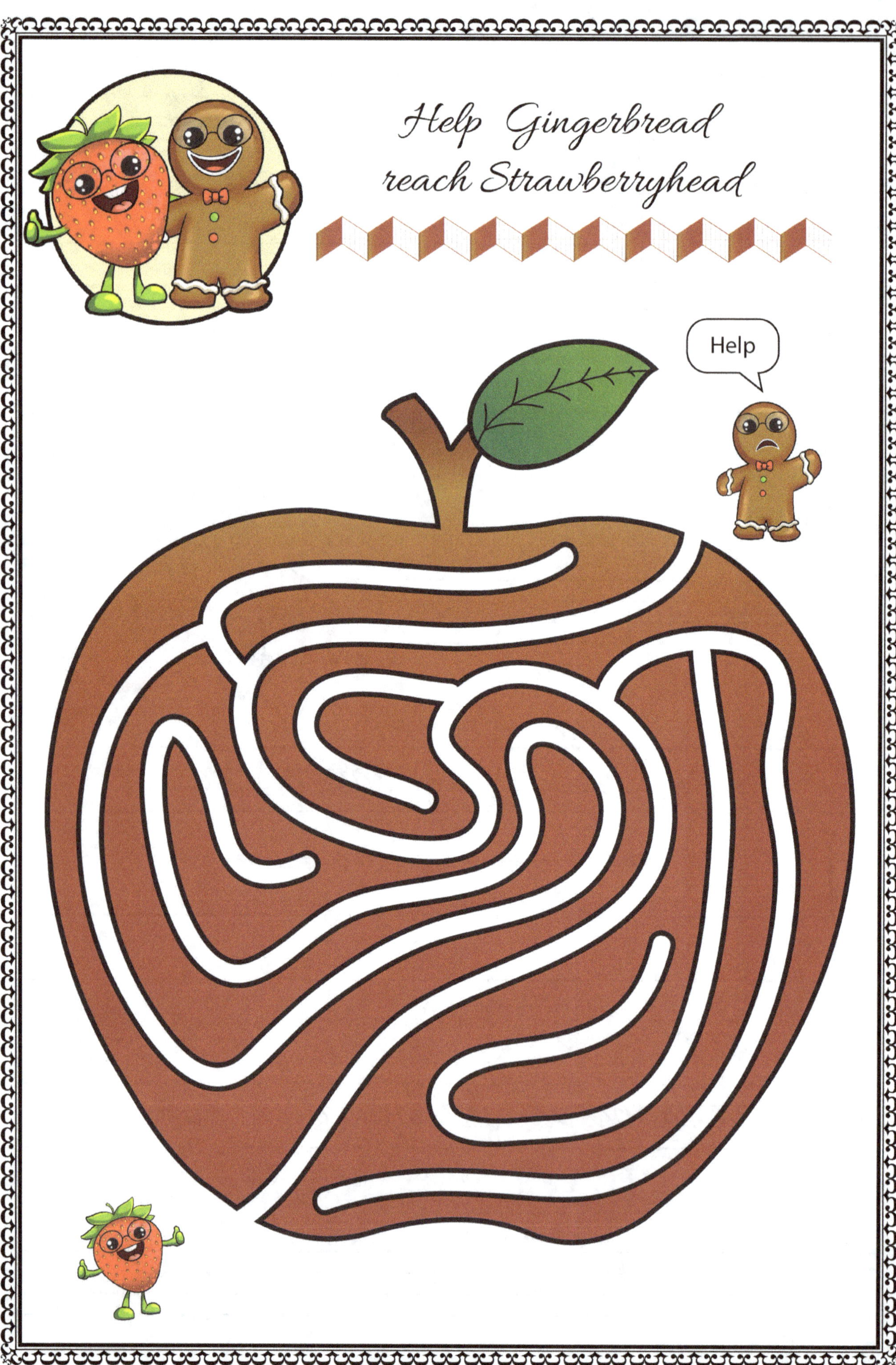

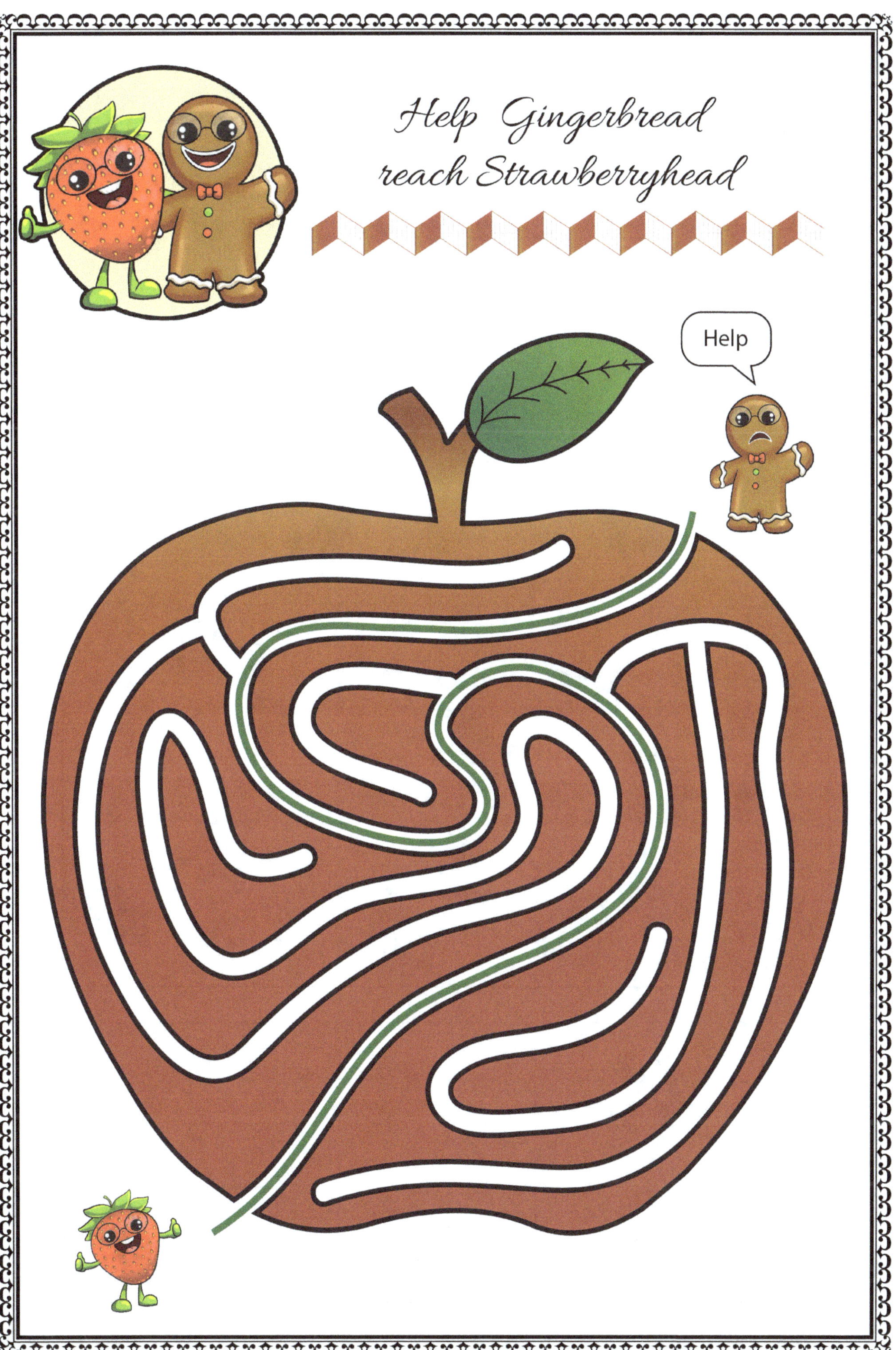

Help  Gingerbread
reach Strawberryhead
Help

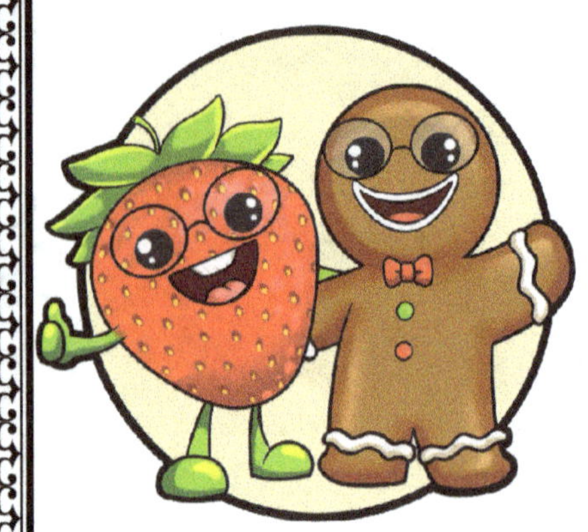

# Find and count the following dogs

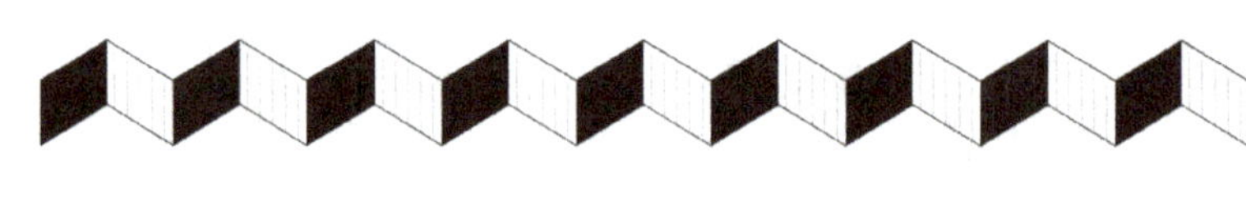

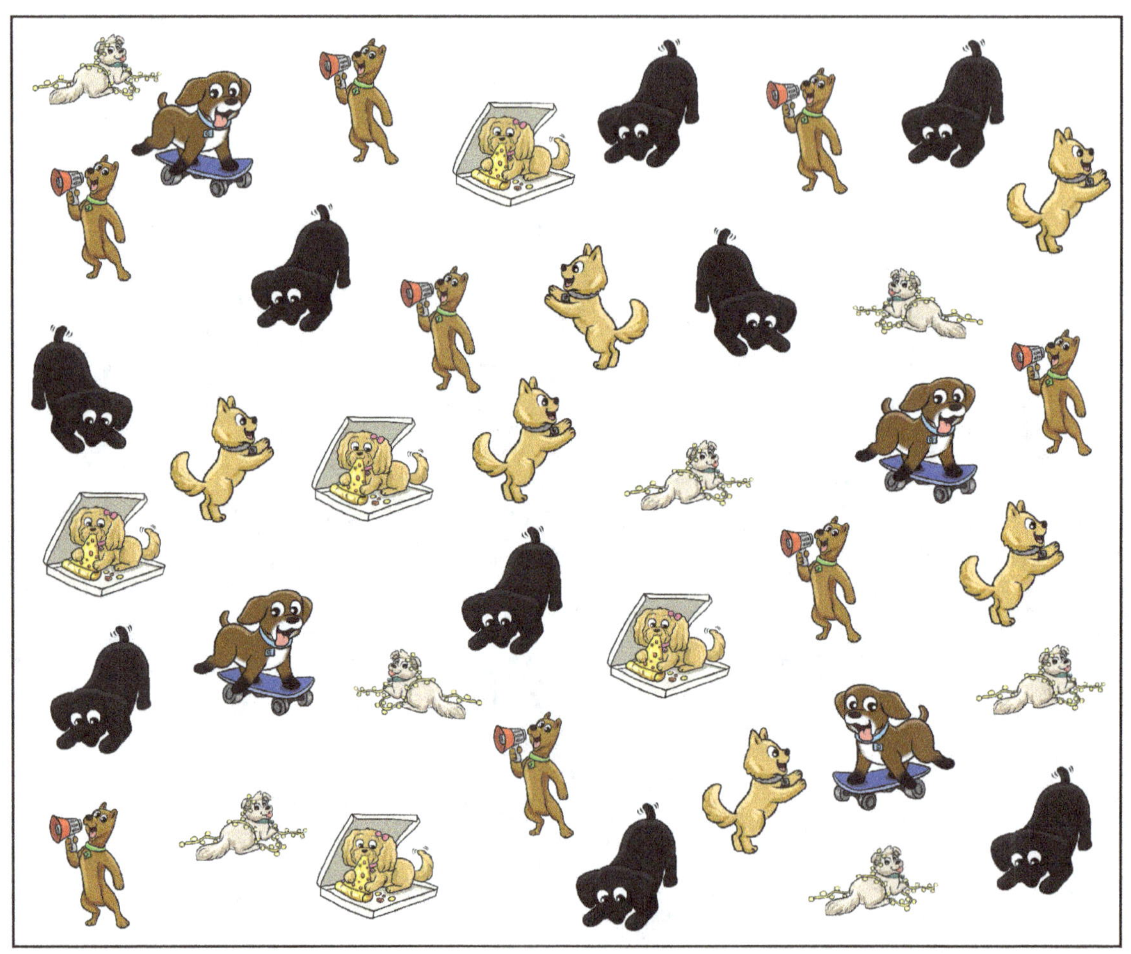

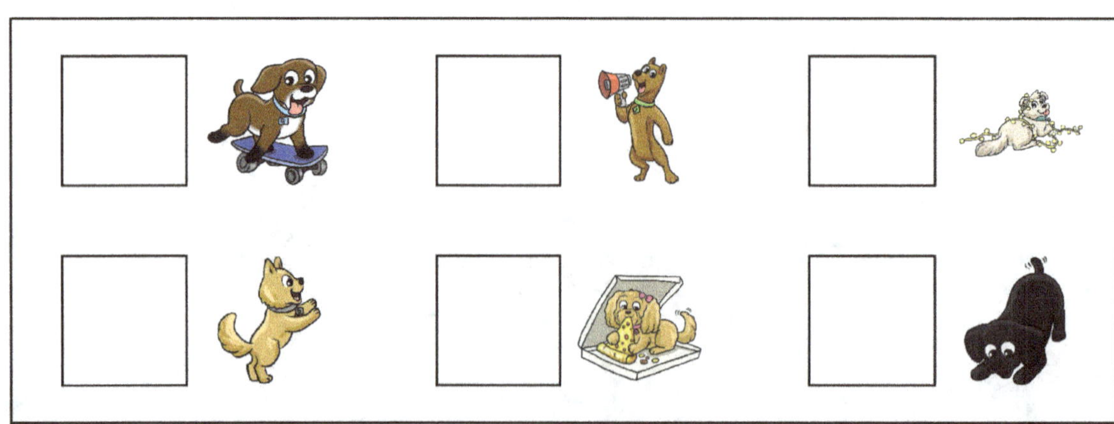

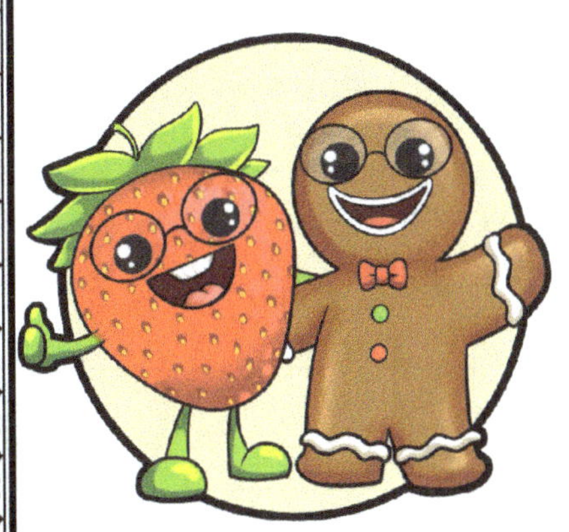


Find and count the following dogs


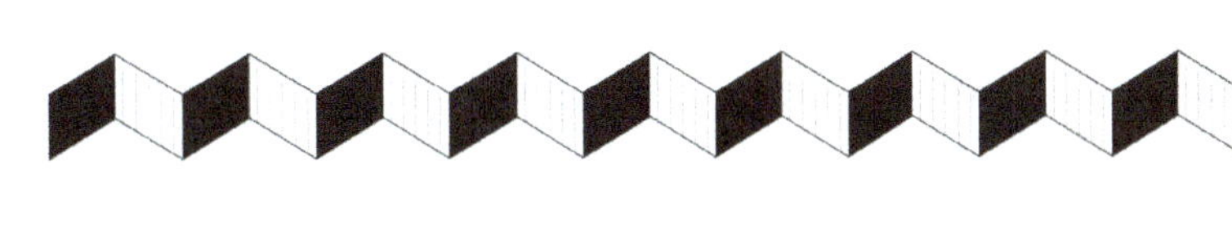

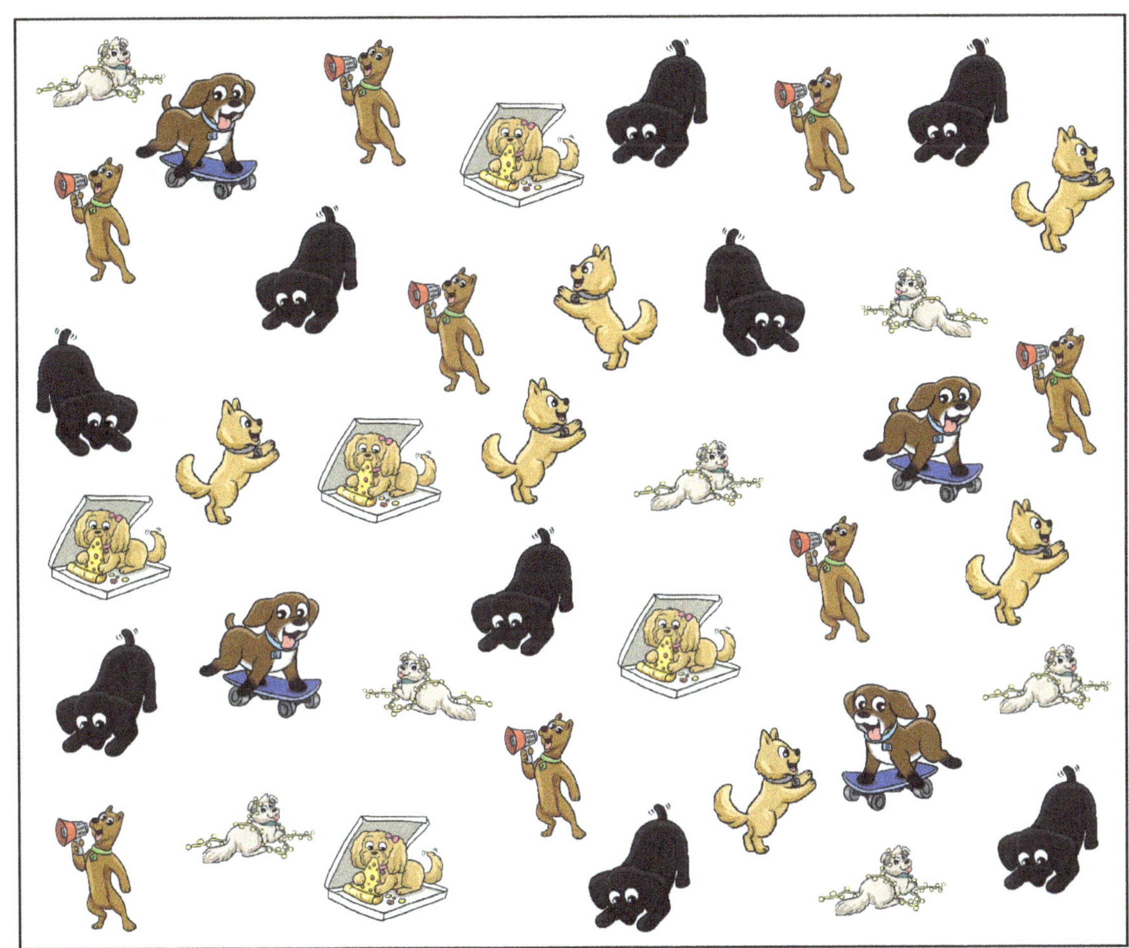

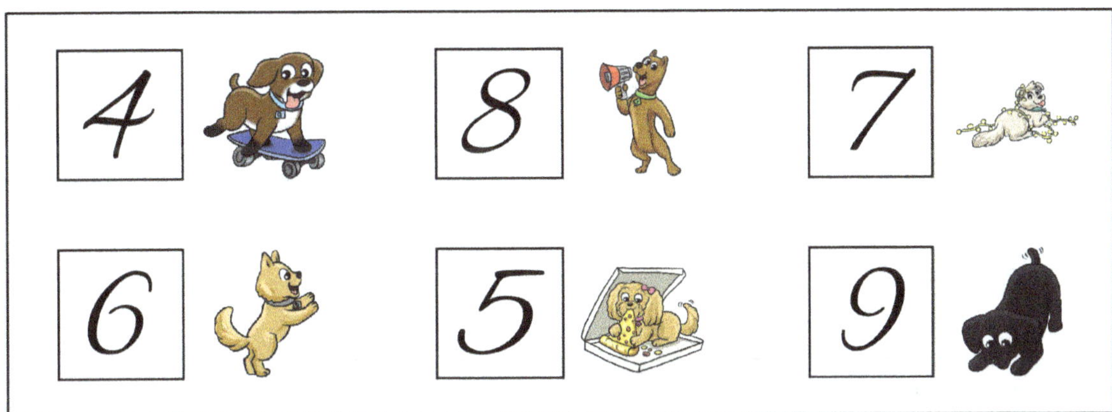

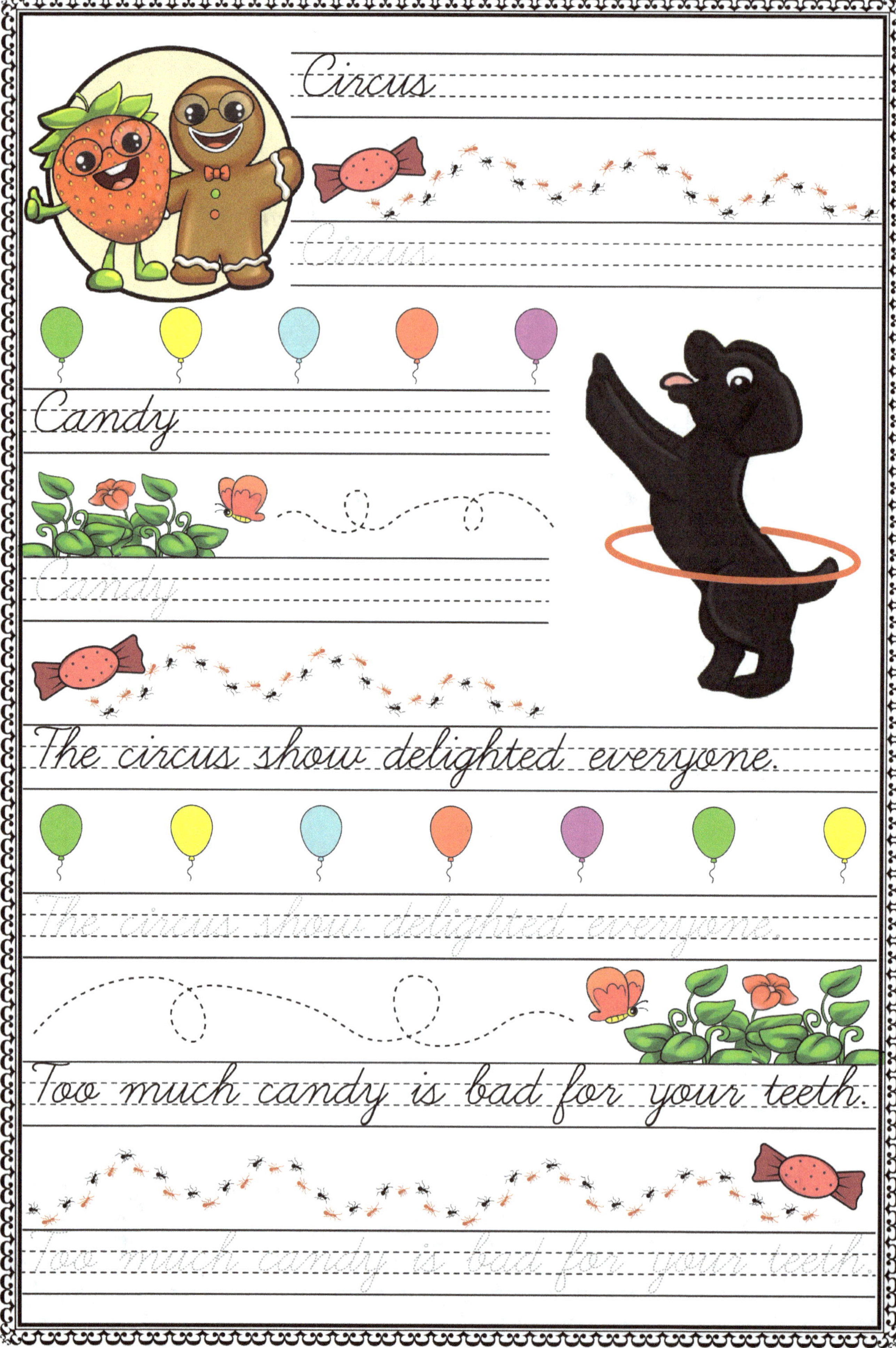

Circus

Circus

Candy

Candy

The circus show delighted everyone.

The circus show delighted everyone.

Too much candy is bad for your teeth.

Too much candy is bad for your teeth.

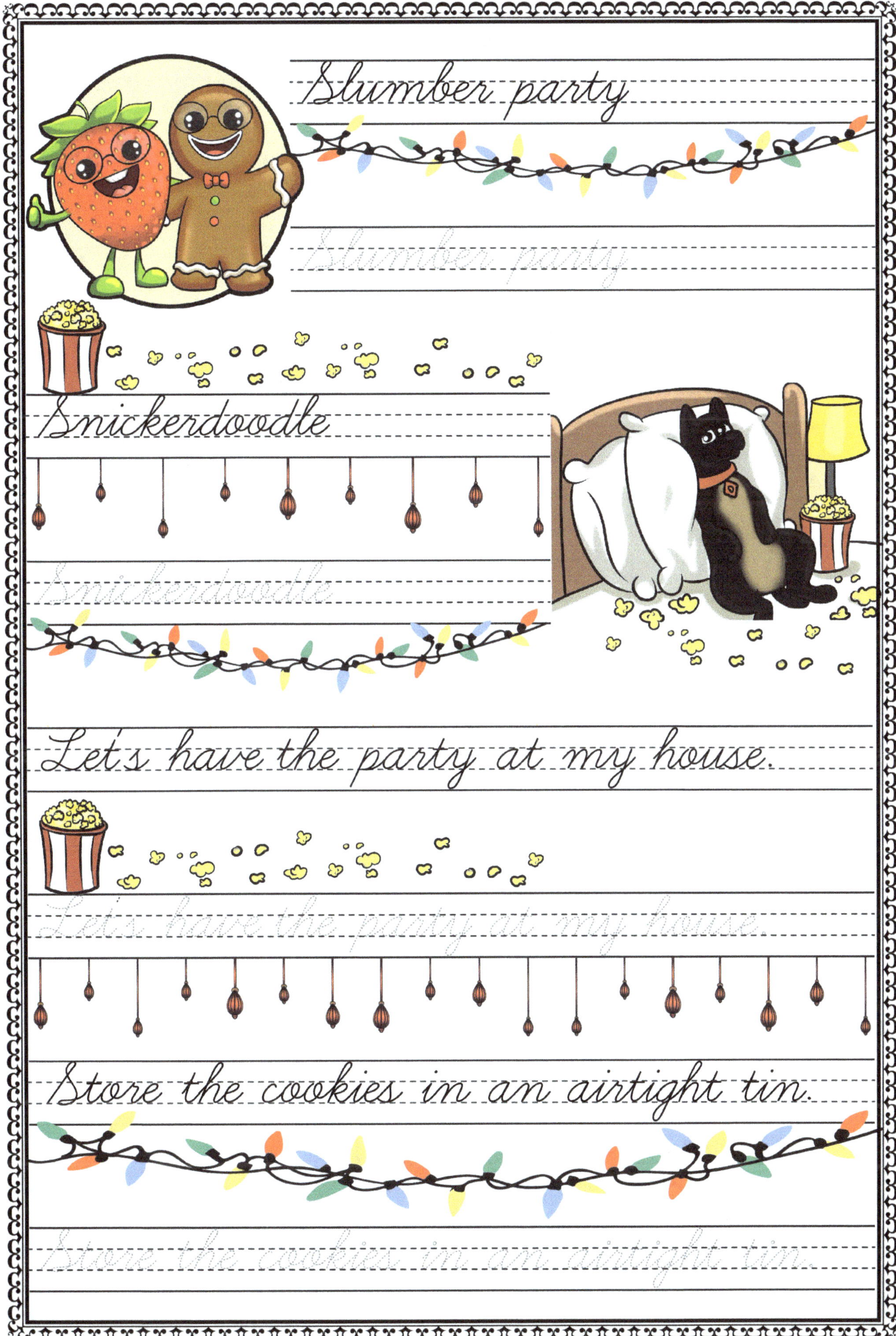

Slumber party

Slumber party

Snickerdoodle

Snickerdoodle

Let's have the party at my house.

Let's have the party at my house.

Store the cookies in an airtight tin.

Store the cookies in an airtight tin.

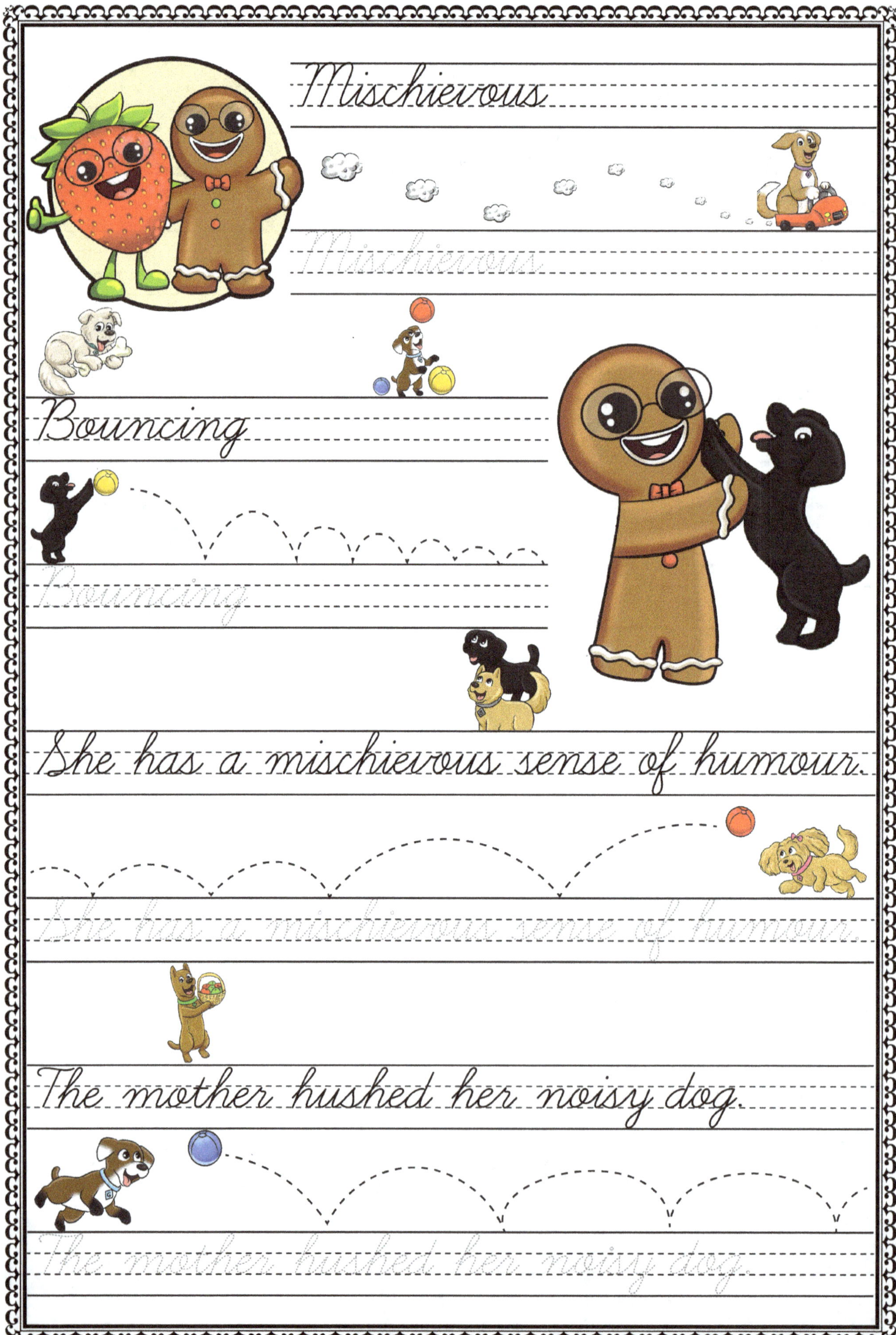

Mischievous

Mischievous

Bouncing

Bouncing

She has a mischievous sense of humour.

She has a mischievous sense of humour.

The mother hushed her noisy dog.

The mother hushed her noisy dog.

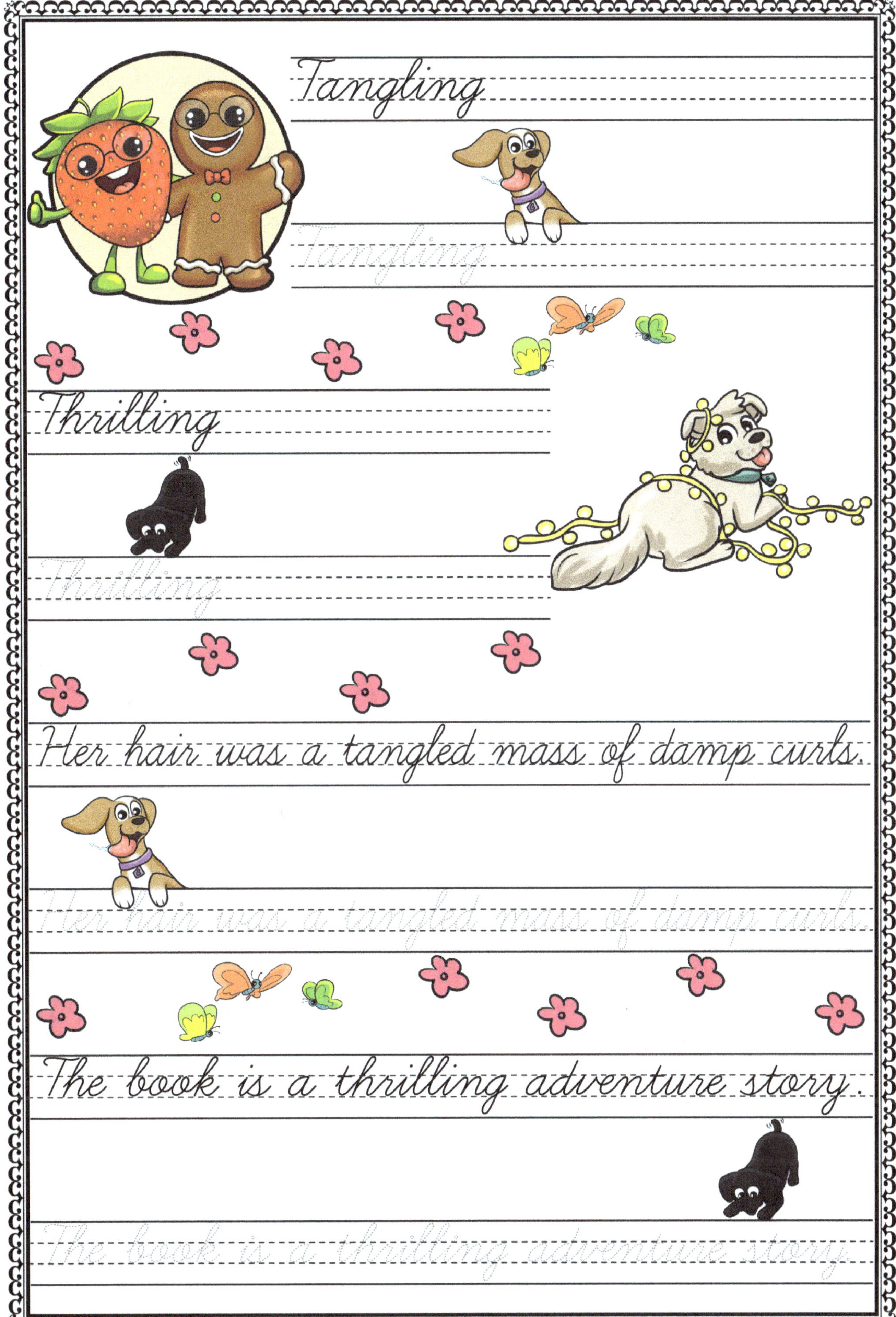

Tangling

Tangling

Thrilling

Thrilling

Her hair was a tangled mass of damp curls.

Her hair was a tangled mass of damp curls.

The book is a thrilling adventure story.

The book is a thrilling adventure story.

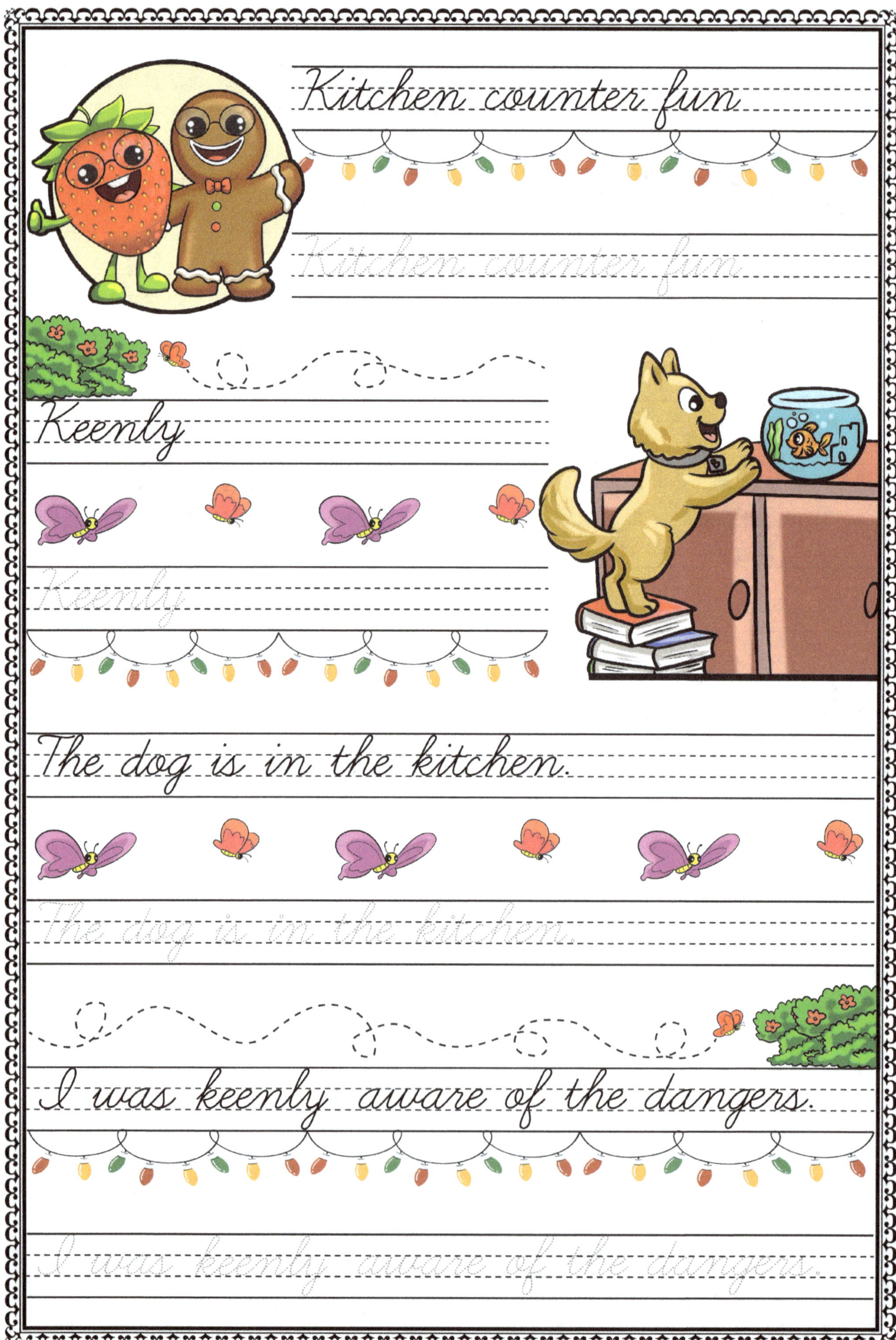

Kitchen counter fun
Kitchen counter fun
Keenly
Keenly
The dog is in the kitchen.
The dog is in the kitchen.
I was keenly aware of the dangers.
I was keenly aware of the dangers.

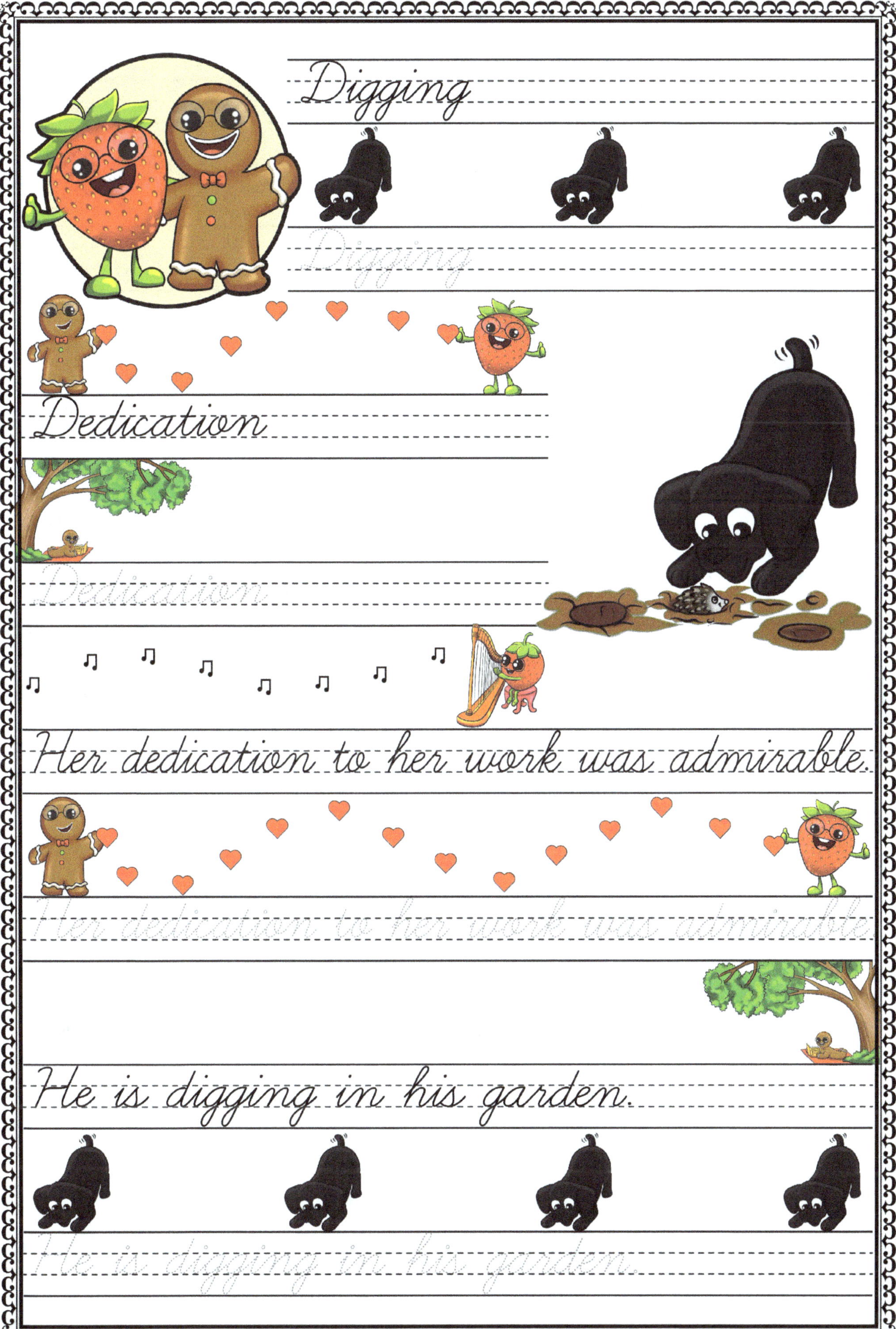

Digging

Digging

Dedication

Dedication

Her dedication to her work was admirable.

Her dedication to her work was admirable.

He is digging in his garden.

He is digging in his garden.

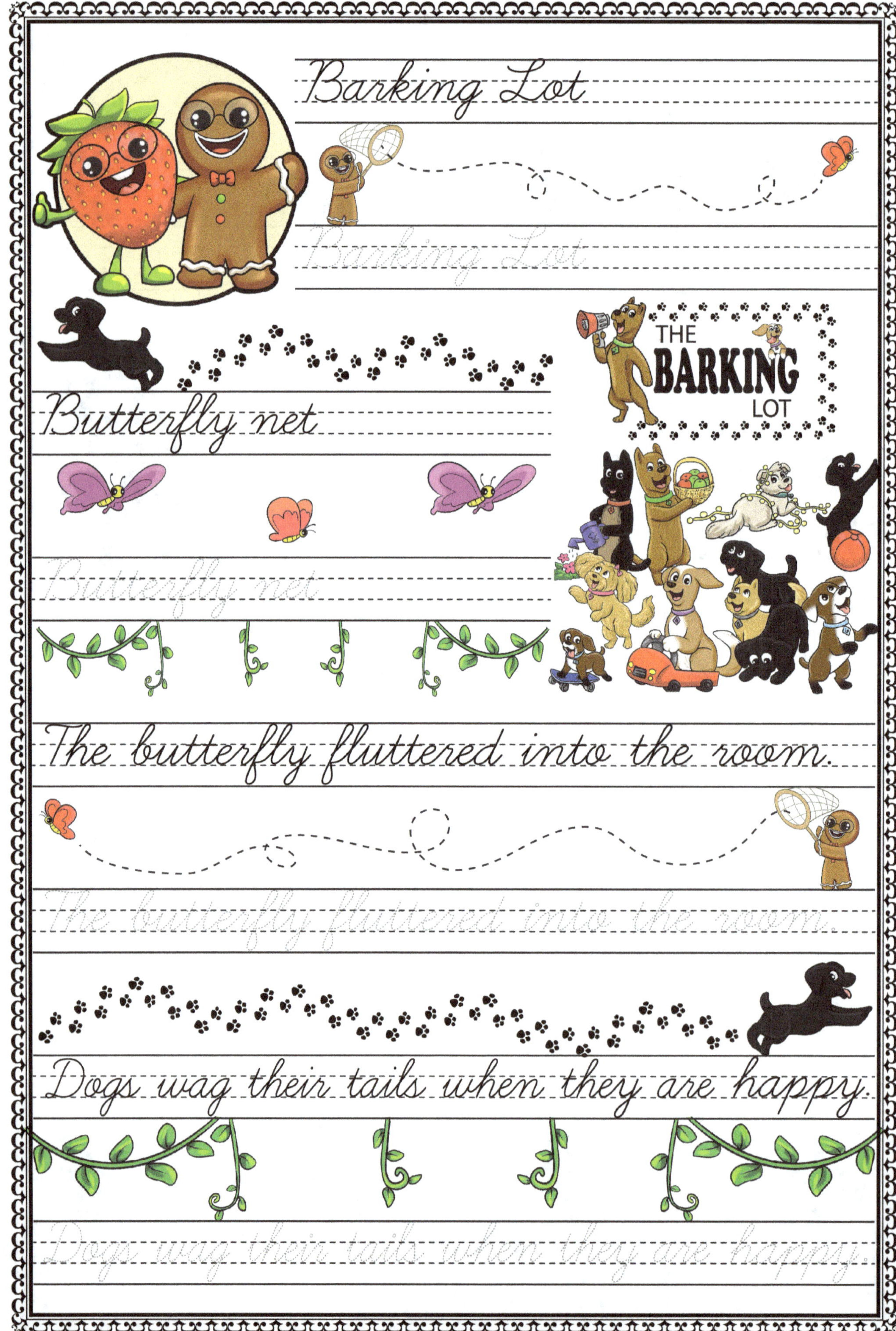

Barking Lot

Barking Lot

Butterfly net

Butterfly net

The butterfly fluttered into the room.

The butterfly fluttered into the room.

Dogs wag their tails when they are happy.

Dogs wag their tails when they are happy.

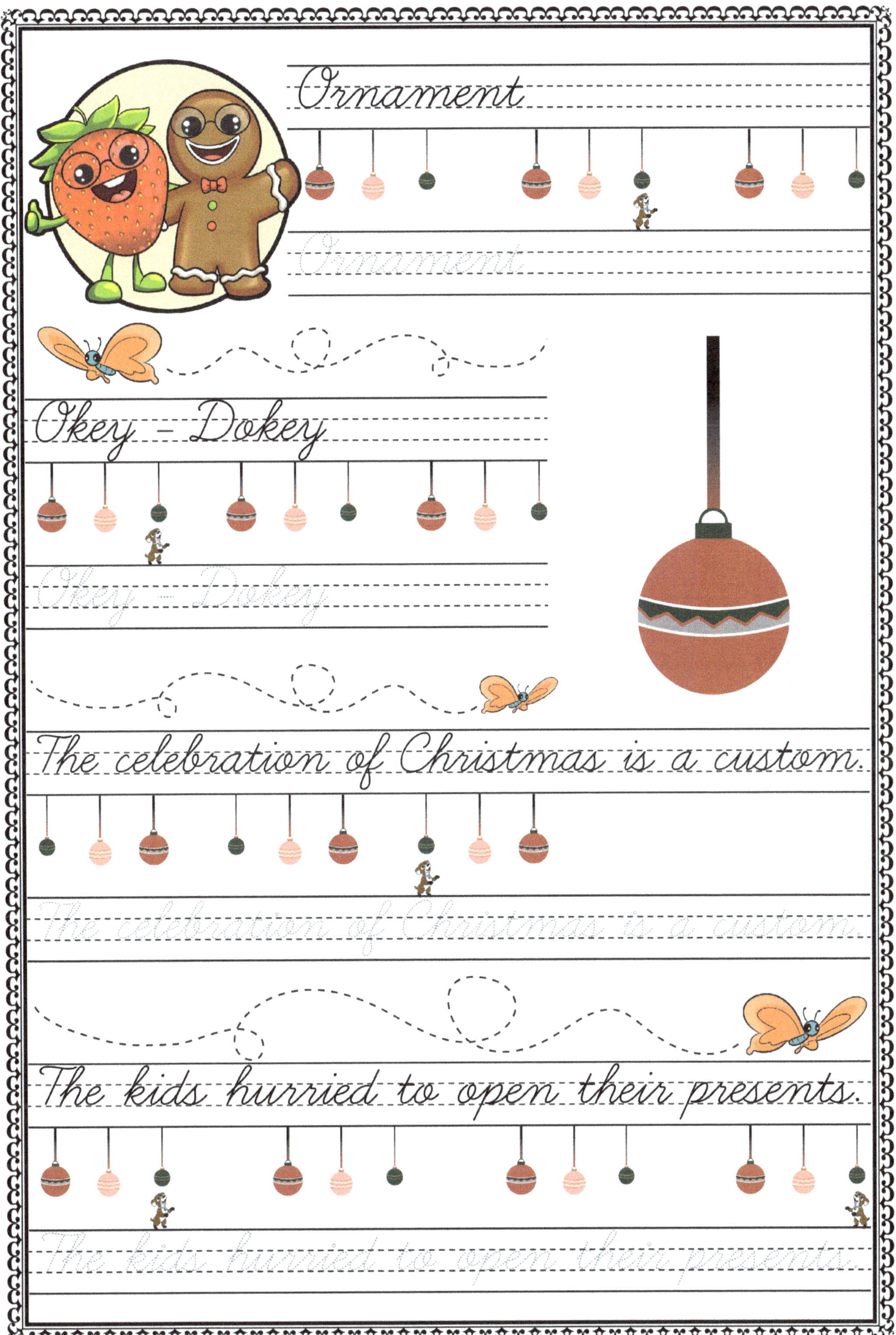

Ornament

*Ornament*

Okey – Dokey

*Okey – Dokey*

The celebration of Christmas is a custom.

*The celebration of Christmas is a custom.*

The kids hurried to open their presents.

*The kids hurried to open their presents.*

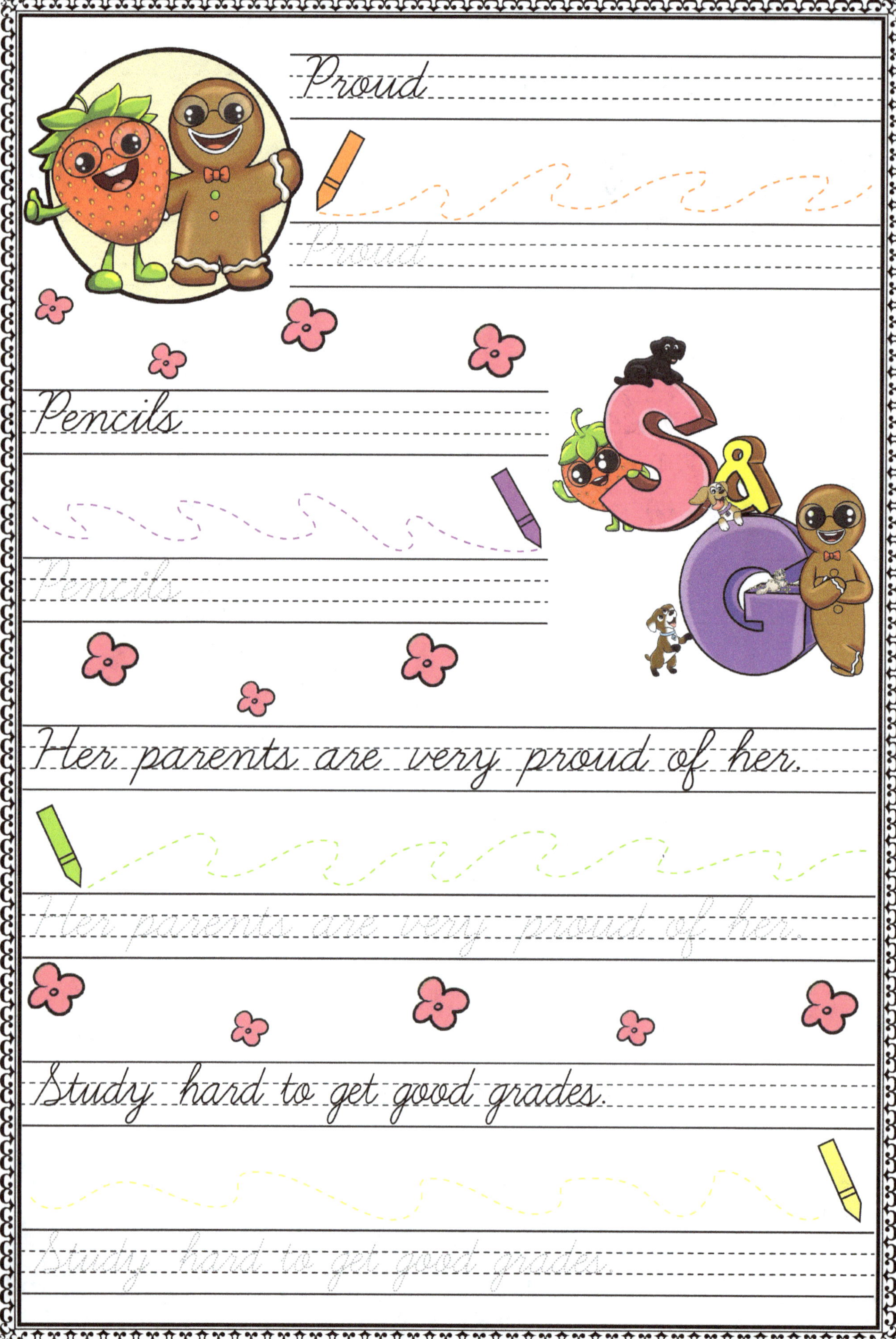

Proud

Proud

Pencils

Pencils

Her parents are very proud of her.

Her parents are very proud of her.

Study hard to get good grades.

Study hard to get good grades.

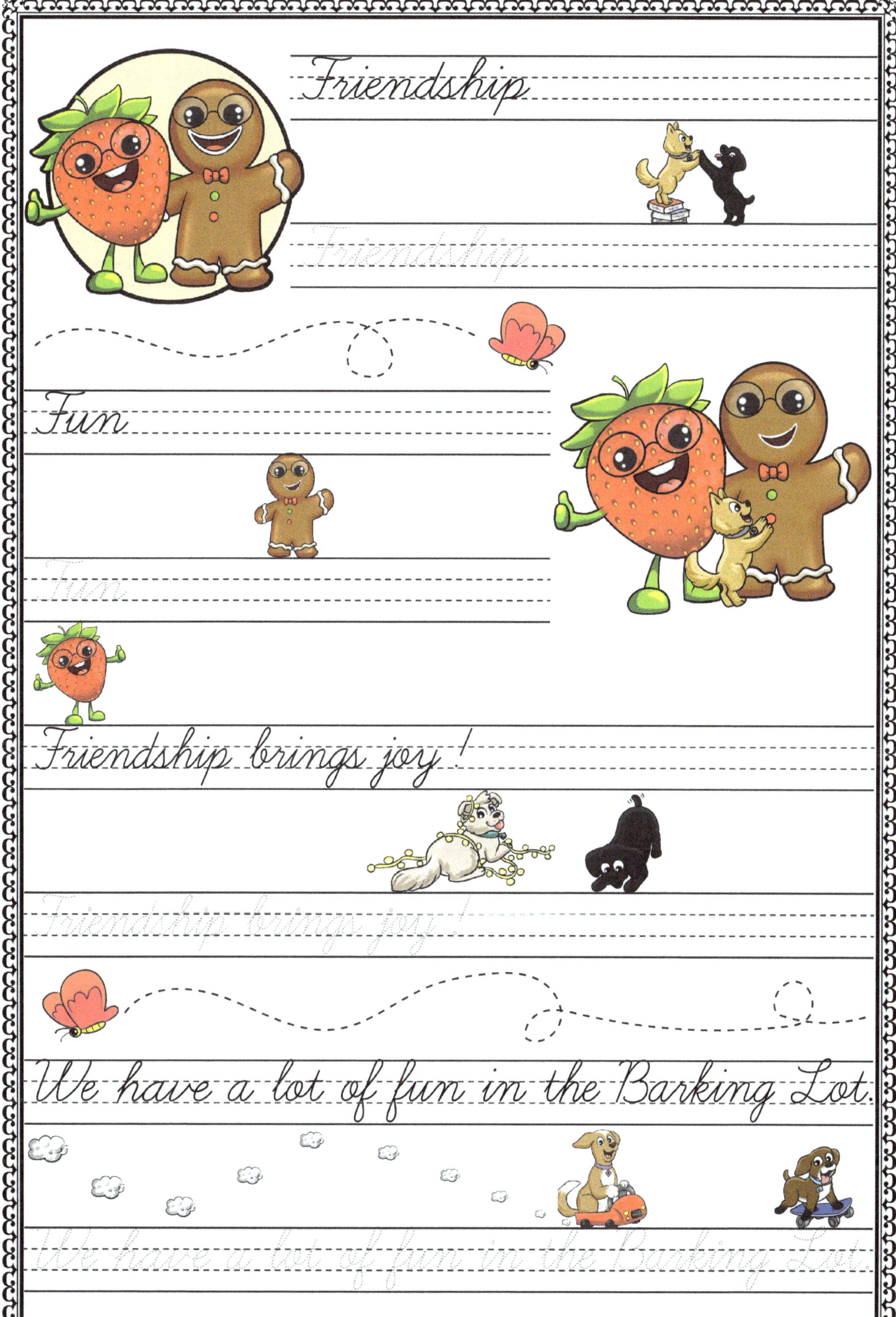

Friendship

Friendship

Fun

Fun

Friendship brings joy!

Friendship brings joy!

We have a lot of fun in the Barking Lot.

We have a lot of fun in the Barking Lot.

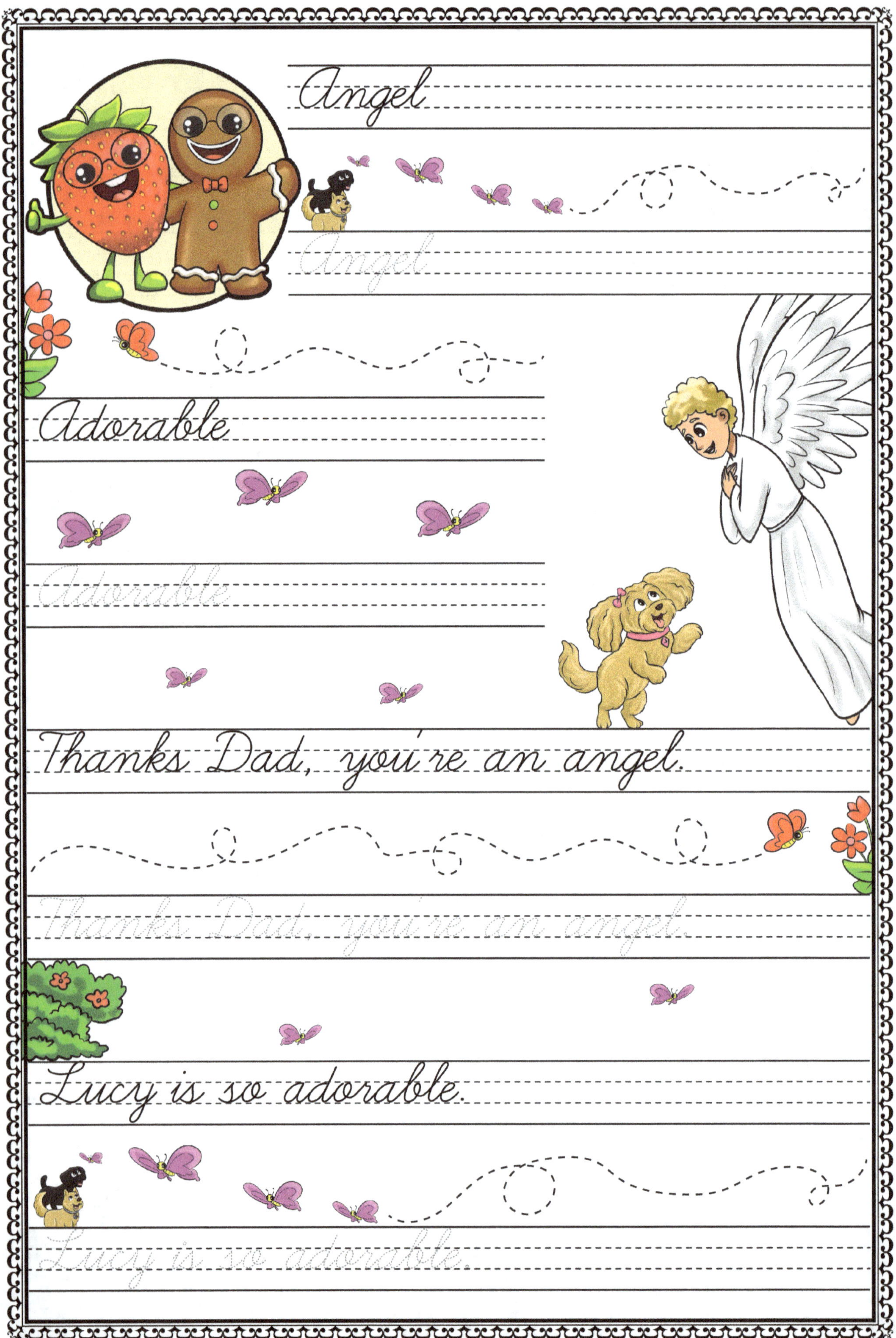

Angel

Angel

Adorable

Adorable

Thanks Dad, you're an angel.

Thanks Dad, you're an angel.

Lucy is so adorable.

Lucy is so adorable.

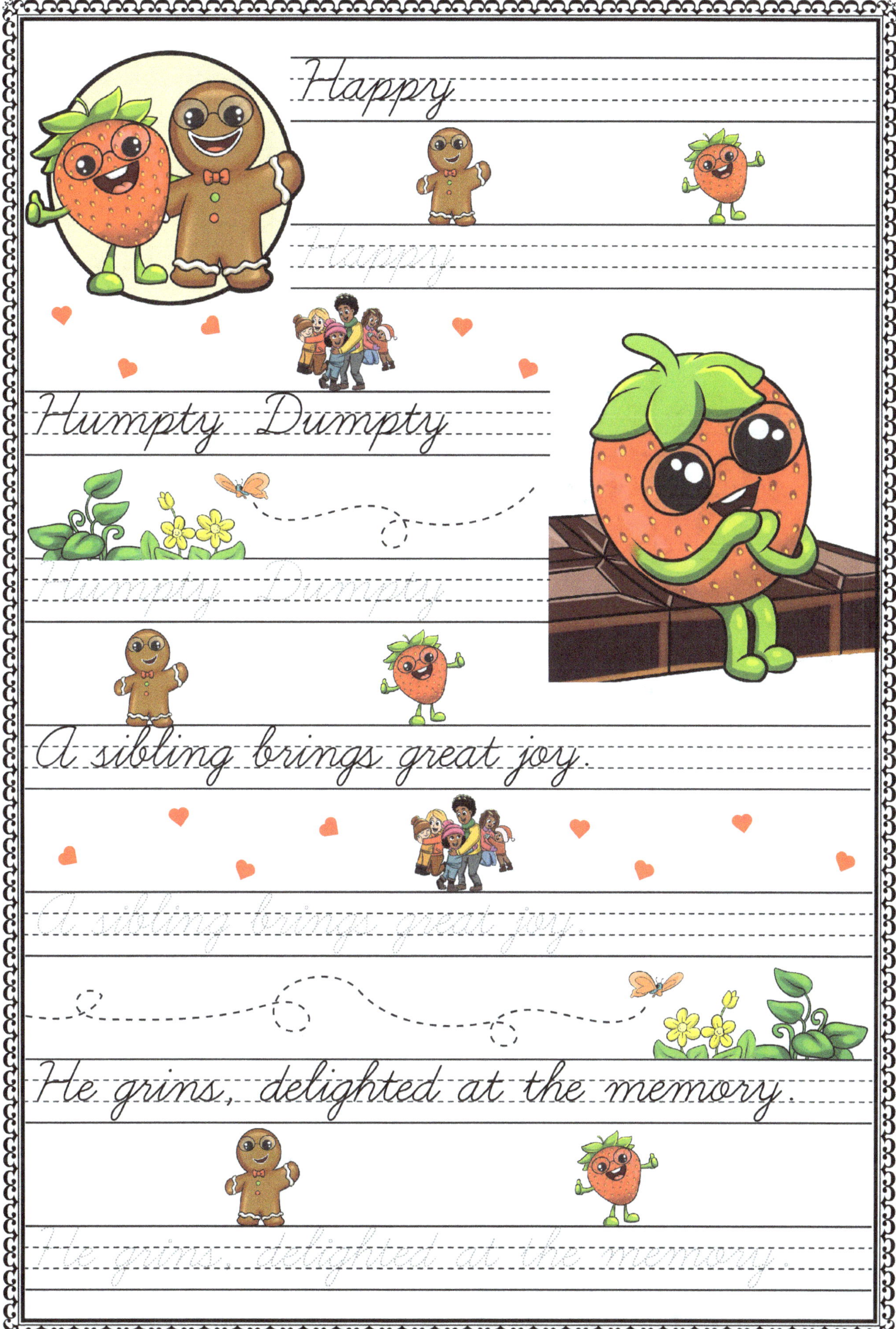

Happy

Happy

Humpty Dumpty

Humpty Dumpty

A sibling brings great joy.

A sibling brings great joy.

He grins, delighted at the memory.

He grins, delighted at the memory.

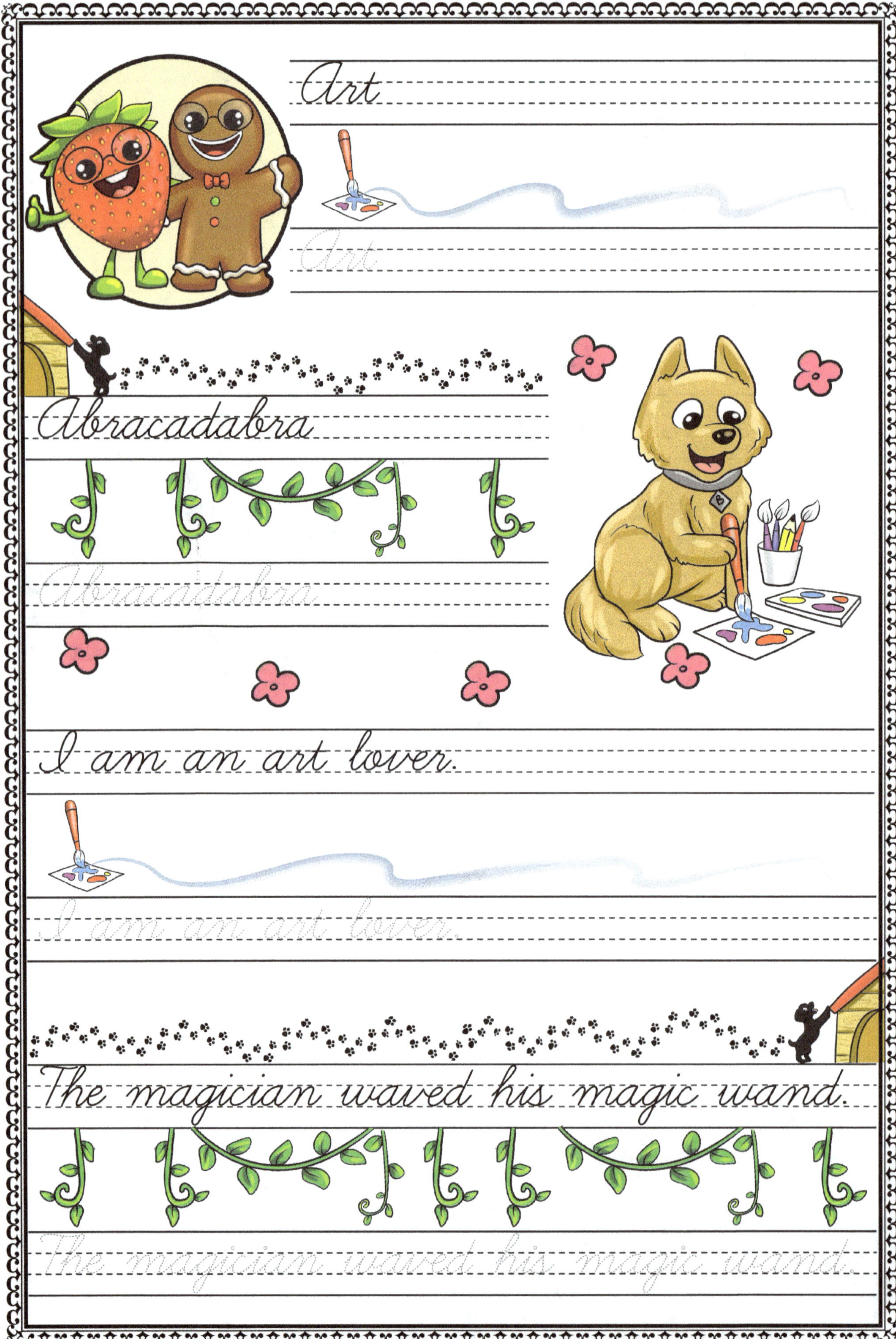

Art

Art

Abracadabra

Abracadabra

I am an art lover.

I am an art lover.

The magician waved his magic wand.

The magician waved his magic wand.

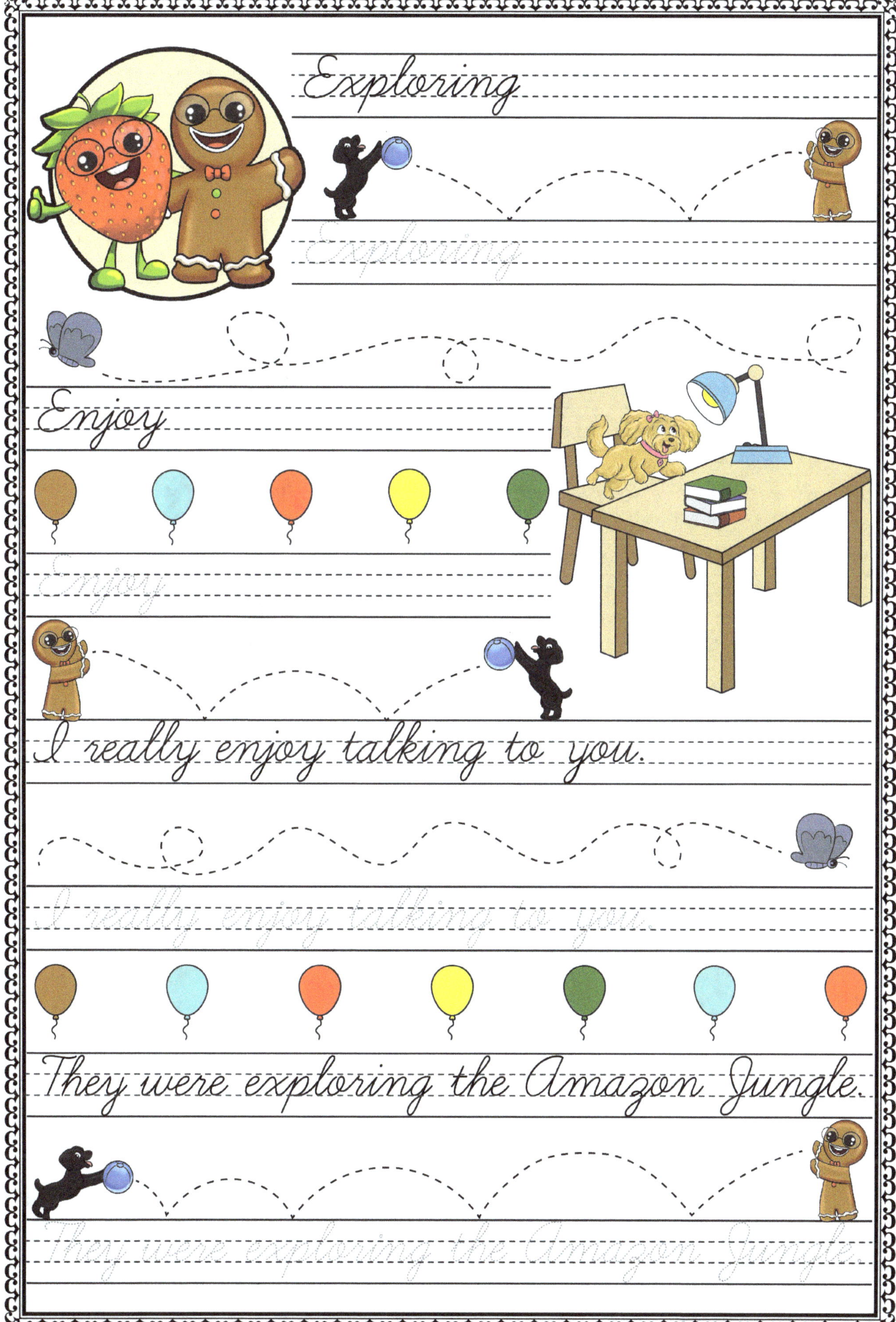

Exploring
Exploring
Enjoy
Enjoy
I really enjoy talking to you.
I really enjoy talking to you.
They were exploring the Amazon Jungle.
They were exploring the Amazon Jungle.

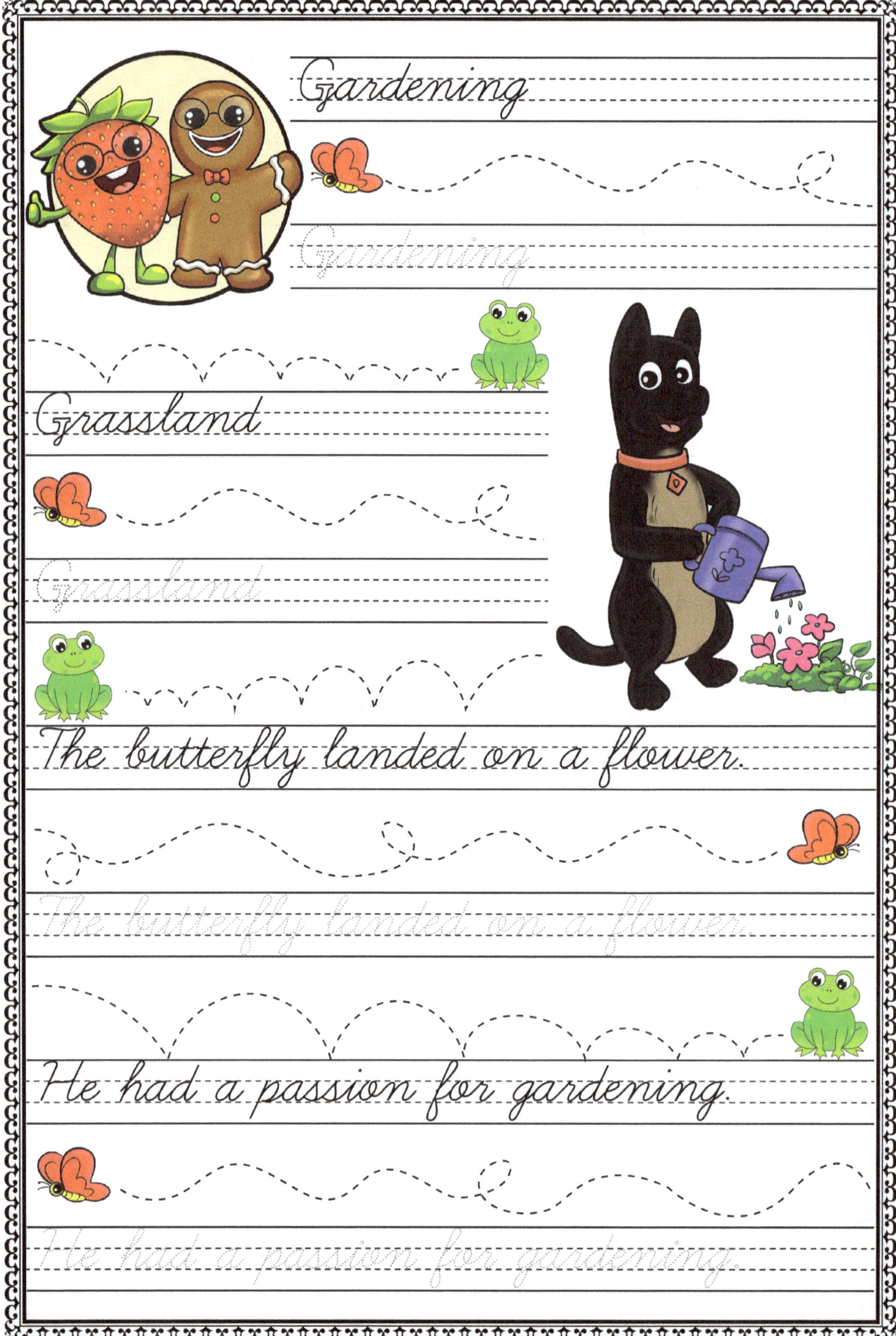

Gardening

Gardening

Grassland

Grassland

The butterfly landed on a flower.

The butterfly landed on a flower.

He had a passion for gardening.

He had a passion for gardening.

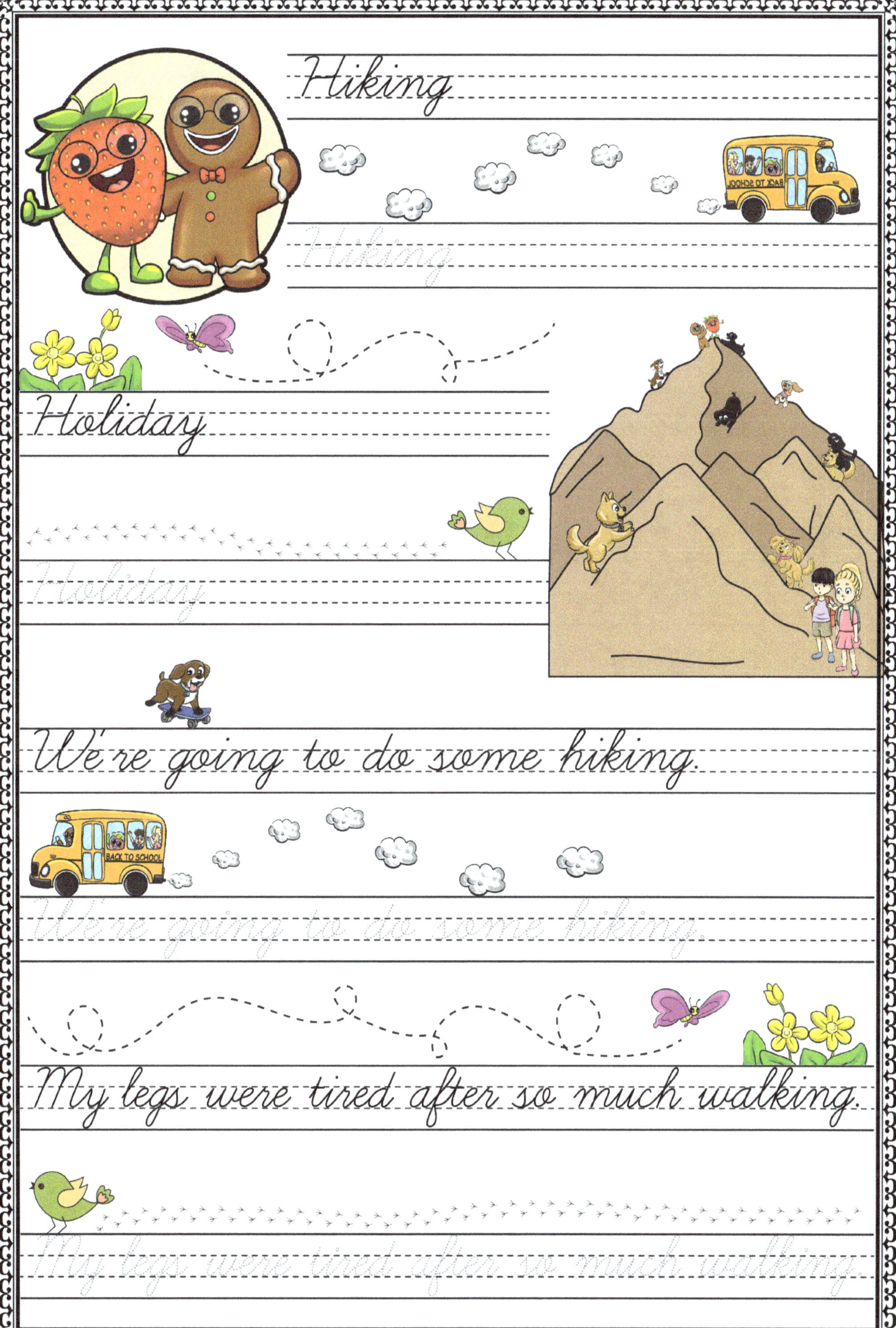

Hiking
Hiking
Holiday
Holiday
We're going to do some hiking.
We're going to do some hiking.
My legs were tired after so much walking.
My legs were tired after so much walking.

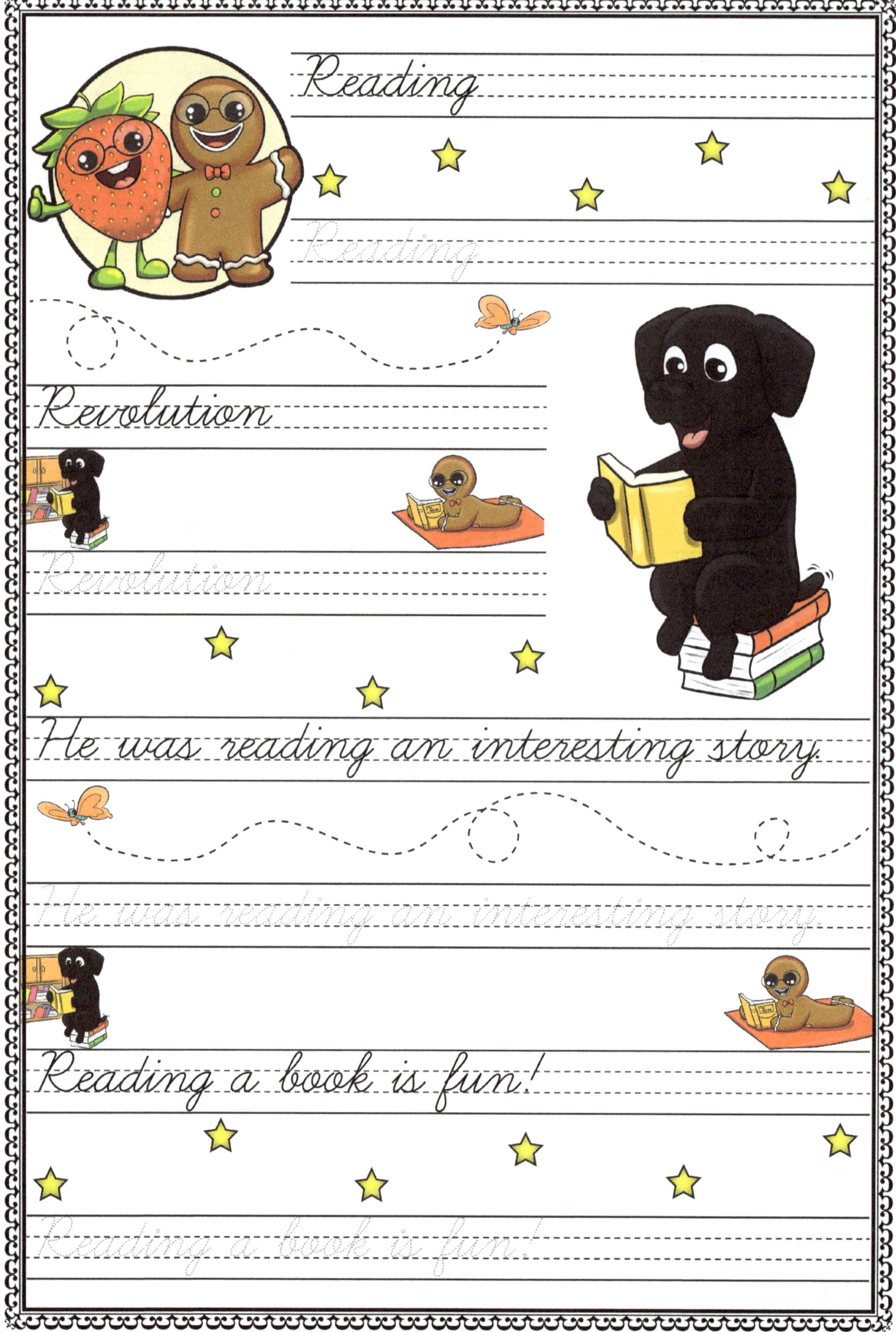

Reading

Reading

Revolution

Revolution

He was reading an interesting story.

He was reading an interesting story.

Reading a book is fun!

Reading a book is fun!

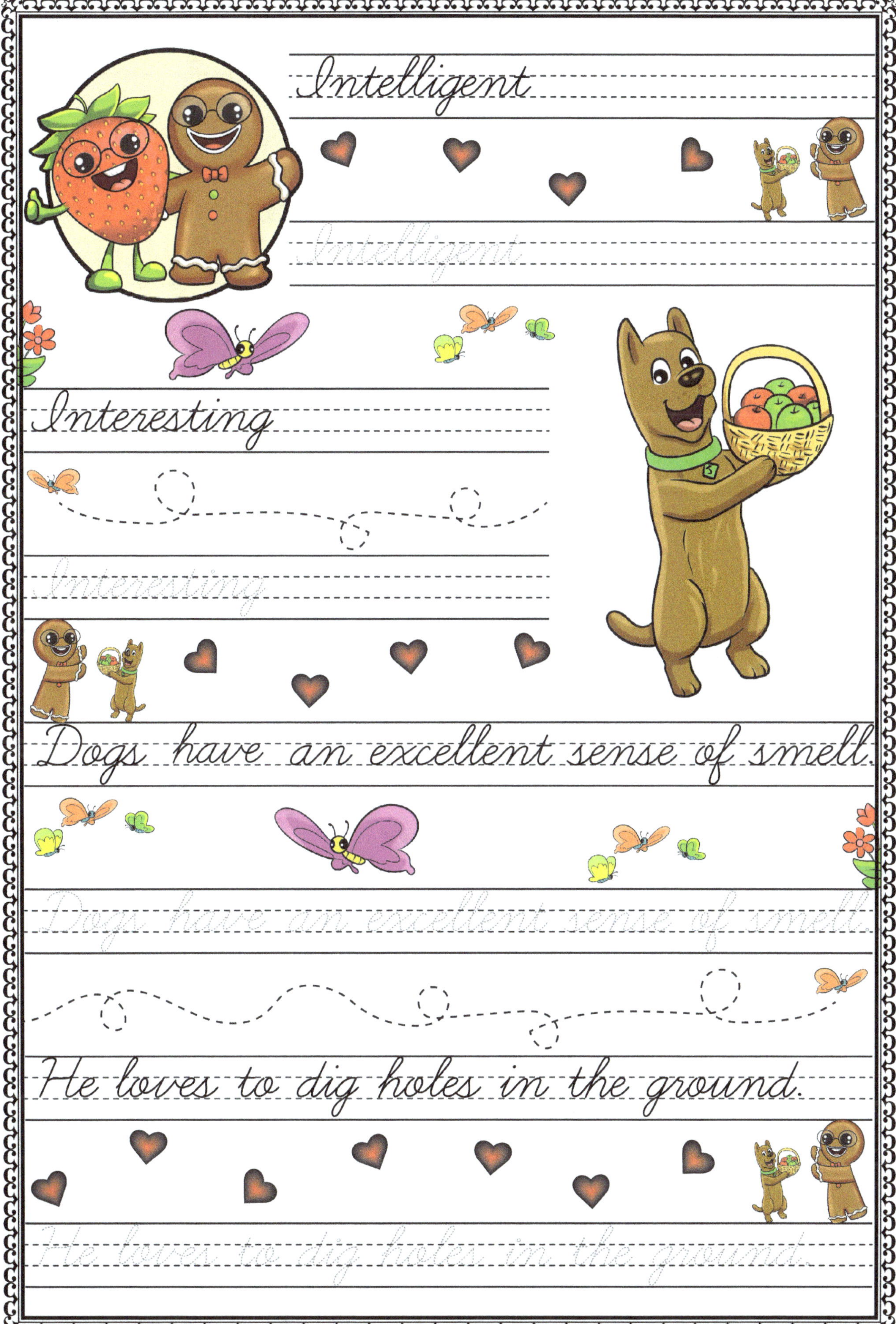

Intelligent

Intelligent

Interesting

Interesting

Dogs have an excellent sense of smell.

Dogs have an excellent sense of smell.

He loves to dig holes in the ground.

He loves to dig holes in the ground.

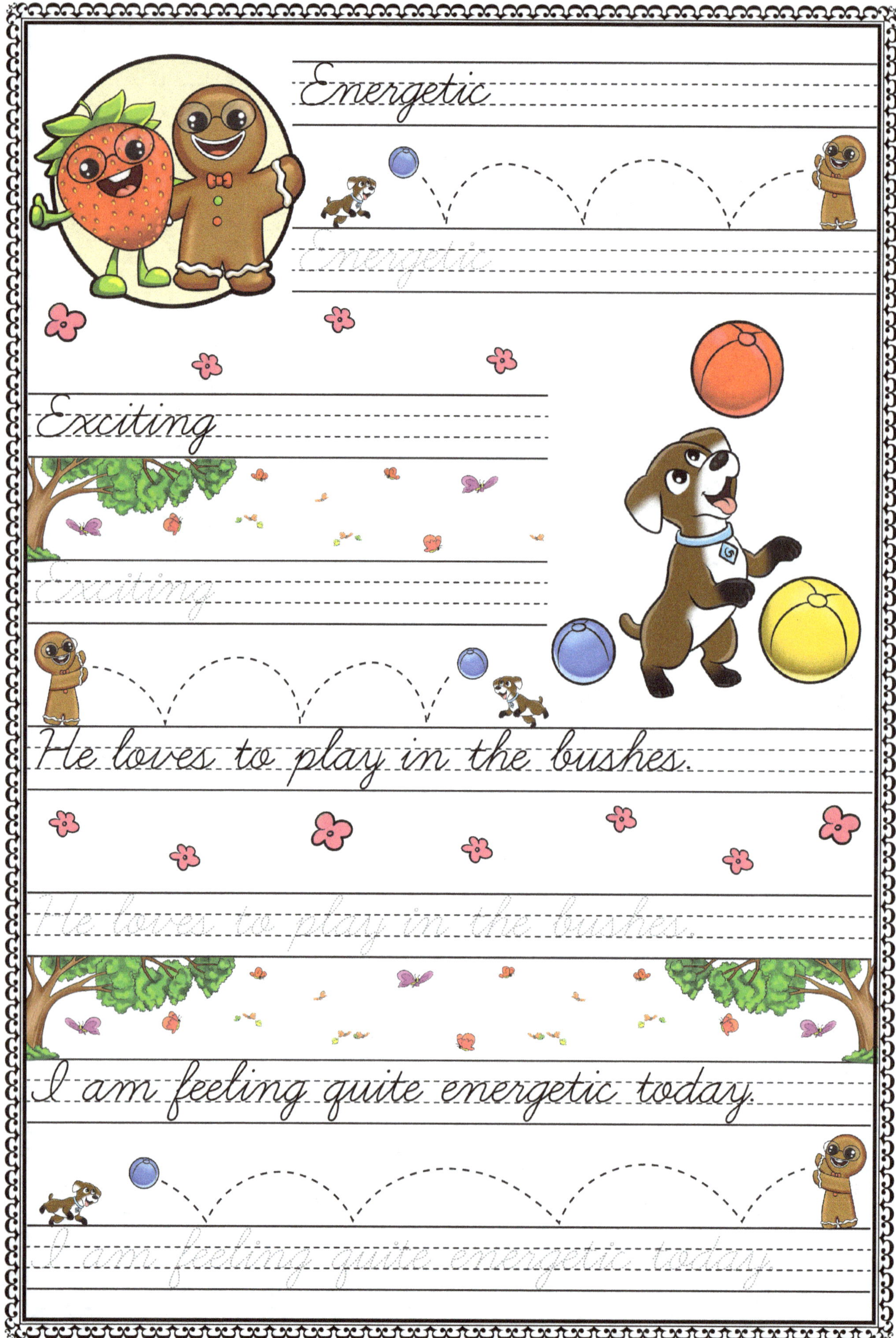

Energetic
Energetic
Exciting
Exciting
He loves to play in the bushes.
He loves to play in the bushes.
I am feeling quite energetic today.
I am feeling quite energetic today.